JOSEPH'S COMPANY

A Boy's Guide to Becoming The Pride of Nations

TOMILOLA OGUNKUNLE
JOANA DZEGBLOR

2 in 1
Edition

Includes
Devotional

JOSEPH'S COMPANY

A Boy's Guide to Becoming The Pride of Nations

This book is presented to:

_____

_____

_____

From:

_____

_____

_____

Dedication

This book is wonderfully dedicated to:

The Holy Spirit–Our consistent Teacher

Every boy who aspires to become the pride of Nations

Contents

Acknowledgements

THIS IS A GOLDEN OPPORTUNITY to express our sincere gratitude to the amazing people God has brought our way through Elegant Initiatives (EI). Parents at EI, thank you for your support in diverse ways; reminding the children of mentoring meetings, book clubs, morning prayer meetings, and most importantly encouraging them to participate in the daily Bible study known as ACAD (A Chapter A Day). We write this with joy, because of the impact EI has made not only in the lives of the children but everyone who is connected to EI in one way or the other globally.

To family and friends who have supported EI with consistent prayers, financially and in other ways, thank you so much. We would not have come this far without your generosity.

A tremendous thank you to our wonderful editorial team; Sammy, Darlington, Judith, Yemi, Juliet and Chidera, for the good work done in proofreading the manuscript.

EI team; Pst Chika & Pst (Mrs) Obioma Edeh, Miss Elizabeth Joshua and Mrs Kehinde Adeniran, thank you so much for being a blessing to this generation.

Josephs and Daniels, our times together will forever be cherished. You encourage and motivate us to keep our feet steady. You are becoming the *Pride of Nations!*

Introduction

Becoming the pride of Nations in a world filled with fear, rivalry, comparison, unhealthy competition and insecurity may be a daunting task for boys. It is saddening, right! But that's the truth. In every home, school, club, organisation, city, state, country, there is always someone or a team that leads, and the leaders are highly respected when they lead with truth, integrity and the power of God.

God has a special purpose for every person He created on earth because He wants His light to shine through the world and make it that pleasant place He created it to be and so His Glory will be revealed in us. And when we are careful to ensure that God's purposes for our lives are accomplished in full, we will attract rewards on earth and in Heaven (eternal reward). That is why God wants you to be intentional about discovering and pursuing your purpose as a 'Joseph' on earth, irrespective of the limitations you may face.

However, figuring out your purpose does not come by just

sitting around your home, eating, playing, watching too much TV and videos, waking up late, being messy and unorganised, and not spending time with God. Figuring out your purpose comes by being intentional about it, so God can work through you. This does not mean you should not play, have fun or rest, it only means you need to have a structure and routine that will guide your choices and activities.

God is ready to walk side by side with you to become a modern day 'Joseph', the pride of Nations, but the question is, 'Are you ready?' Hear what He says, (you can insert your name where you see Jerusalem).

> *"Because I love Zion, I will not keep still. Because my heart yearns for Jerusalem, I cannot remain silent. I will not stop praying for [him], until [his] righteousness shines like the dawn, and [his] salvation blazes like a burning torch. The nations will see your righteousness. World leaders will be blinded by your glory. And you will be given a new name by the Lord's own mouth. The Lord will hold you in his hand for all to see a splendid crown in the hand of God. O Jerusalem, I have posted watchmen on your walls; they will pray day and night, continually. Take no rest, all you who pray to the Lord. Give the Lord no rest until He completes his work, **until He makes Jerusalem the pride of the earth.**"*
>
> *—Isaiah 62:1–4,6–7*

It is with great joy in our hearts to write this book. We are so convinced that the treasure you are about to discover in this book will help you to emerge as the *Pride of Nations.*

PART ONE

Joseph's Treasure

Tomiann's Dream

"I woke up from a dream on 10th June, 2019. In the dream I was given something of great value by someone I respect so much. As I was thinking about the dream, God made me realise that the person was sent to me by Him. As my usual practice, I grabbed my 'Vision Book', where I document my visions and dreams, and I wrote my dream in it.

Afterwards, I asked God to give me the interpretation of the dream and He did. I didn't waste time, as the Holy Spirit downloaded the interpretation to me. I wrote every bit of what I received and I will be sharing some with you, so you can have a better understanding of the first three chapters of this book."

Interpretation of My Dream

- The gift is a treasure.
- It must be cherished and preserved at all costs.
- It must not be wasted or lost.
- As much as it is being cared for, it can't run out.
- It is the provision to fulfil destiny.
- Out of it, nations shall be blessed.
- It will bring peace and rest.
- God is the giver of all things and all gratitude must be given to Him.

As I was meditating on the interpretation, I was directed by the Holy Spirit to this Scripture:

> *"I will give you hidden treasures, riches stored in secret places, so that you may know that I am the LORD, the God of Israel, who summons you by name."*
>
> *–Isaiah 45:3*

My life has been transformed by that encounter and your life will also be transformed as you discover and cherish the 'Treasure' that will be given in this section.

In this section, we will be discussing:

ONE

Joseph's Time

And of the children of Issachar, which were men that had understanding of the time, to know what Israel ought to do.

—I Chronicles 12:32a

Ten Facts About Time

Have you ever sat down to think about 'Time'?
1.   Time is a treasure.
2.   Everyone has a measure of time.
3.   Everyone has 24 hours to spend in a day.
4.   You can't slow time down.
5.   You can take charge of your time.
6.   You can do anything with your time.
7.   What you spend your time on is your choice.

8. Time is limited.
9. You are accountable for your time.
10. God controls the timer for your life. He stops the timer when your time is up.

Understanding Of Time

Having an understanding of time early in your life and doing all it takes to use the time you have been given wisely gives you speed to do what you have to do and to do it well. It makes it look like you have 48 hours a day while others think they have less than 24 hours a day. At the time when David was about to be enthroned as king, people were in a state of confusion about what to do but the children of Issachar knew what to do. Why? Because they had an understanding of that period.

A survey was carried out about the time people have and how they spent it on what they had to do. People of different ages were sampled and placed in groups of 10. Here is the result of the survey:

Age Range	No Time	Less Time	Enough Time
7–11 years	3	2	5
12–17 years	4	3	3
18–25 years	6	2	2

Which category do you belong to? You need to be honest with yourself.

A common statement often made by people who claim to have no or less time is, "I don't have time." With the facts you now know about time, is it true that they don't have time?

It is so interesting the things we found out in this survey from children, teenagers and young adults who claimed they had no or less time to spend. Those things are called 'time stealers' and we will talk about them later in this chapter.

Looking at the few who genuinely said they had enough time for their tasks, we could see a difference in their results. These are the few who not only understand the facts about time, but they know what to do with their time and they also do it.

Do you need enough time to do all that you have to do? Or do you have enough time already and you desire to sustain it so as to be able to accommodate greater opportunities that come your way? To meet your desire, you need to maximise your time.

How Can You Gain More Time?

Teach us to use wisely all the time we have.
—Psalm 91:12

1. You need wisdom

To gain more time, the first thing you need to do is to ask

God to teach you how to use the time He has given you. You need wisdom and that wisdom only comes from the One who created you and gave you time. If you ask Him for wisdom, He will give you because He is the Ultimate Source of wisdom.

2.   You need to write down your goal

A goal simply means something that you want to achieve. *For example, the writers of the book in your hand had a goal to write and publish it at a set time.* When you have a goal, it guides you to plan and take actions.

3.   You need to plan

Remember, having a goal will motivate you to put a plan in place on how to achieve your goal. *For instance, the writers of this book went ahead to decide on how many chapters to write, the titles, duration to spend writing daily and so on.* Mind map is an excellent way of laying out your plan. "Mind Map for Kids" written by Tony Buzan, is a good book that teaches the shortcut to getting things done excellently. You can apply the knowledge from it to planning anything you need to do.

Planning is very important because if you don't plan your day, someone else will plan it for you. If you don't learn to take charge of your time, it will be controlled by someone or something else.

4.   You need to take action

Planning prompts you into action.

It is good to have your goal and your plan ready before taking action. There are lots of people who don't really have specific goals and spend their entire lives planning. Some people have goals but do not plan before taking action. The third category are the people who keep doing something but when you ask them what they want to achieve, that is their goal, they don't really have one. The last group of people are those who take **goal**, **plan** and **action** 'G–P–A' seriously and this is where you are advised to be.

5.   You need to be consistent with your actions

G–P–A will guide you a lot in anything you set your mind to do. However, CONSISTENCY with your G–P–A is your secret code to SUCCESS. There are times you would not feel like doing what you plan to do but whenever you remember your goal, jump up into action. The only time you might not work according to your plan is if you are really not able to, especially when you are tired or you need to do something else that is more important.

6.   You need to review your G–P–A

Checking if what you are doing is what you are meant to do from time to time is very important. How do you do this? Just as you asked God to give you wisdom on how to spend your time, that is the same way you ask Him to guide you to do the right thing at the right time. See what *Psalm 32:8* says–

> *"I will instruct you and teach you in the way you should go; I will counsel you with my loving eye on you."*

God doesn't want you to waste the time He gave you, so He will not only give you wisdom, He will also guide you if you ask Him to. You can also speak to your parents, Bible study teacher or your mentor, if you need further help.

To be consistent at something (e.g. learning a skill or studying for examinations) may not be easy but success will not happen without consistency.

The writers of this book have had to work on some projects together and there were times we had to discontinue some projects because we realised God was not guiding us in that direction. There were other times we had to change our plans and start all over again. You might also need to stop what you are doing currently if you need to and you might need to start all over. Ending well should be your focus.

7.   You need to guard your time

Spend your time on things that matter to God and on things

you are meant to do. Simple! Spend time on things that are worthwhile and productive. The time unwisely used is the time the devil takes advantage of. Give no room to the devil by doing whatever it takes to guard your time.

Your Time Is In Your Hand

You can control your time. Yes! The time the Owner gave you, before He takes it back. You can take charge of your time; it's right in your hand. Let's look at some of the ways the virtuous woman takes charge of her time, as seen in Proverbs 31.

- She's up before dawn.
- She organizes her day.
- First thing in the morning, she dresses for work, rolls up her sleeves.
- She's eager to get started.
- She senses the worth of her work, and is in no hurry to call it quits for the day.

Time Stealers and Wasters

Things that get in the way of your G–P–A to distract you can be referred to as 'Time Stealers or Time Wasters'. They are things that drift into your mind to hinder you from doing the things you set your mind to do. Joyce Meyer, one of the world's leading practical Bible teachers, calls them *'Mind Benders'* in her book 'Battlefield of the Mind for Kids'. The Bible also has a word for time stealers–*'Weight'*. Let's look at it:

> *"Let us strip off every **weight** that slows us down,*
> *especially the sin that so easily trips us up"*
> *–Hebrews 12:1b*

Below are some of the time stealers and wasters that you need to let go off or control.

Time Stealers	Time Wasters
Lack of G–P–A (Goal–Plan–Action)	Poor Planning
Laziness	Excessive talks or chats
Wrong Association	TV
Procrastination	Social Media
Ungodly habits	Gossiping
Lack of Discipline	Day–dreaming

When you lose your time to time stealers, it's hard to get it back. When time wasters get in your way, you would end up being stressed, because you chose something not important over what is important. Time stealers and wasters are enemies you need to deal with, if you desire to fulfil the purpose of God for your life and become the Joseph after His heart.

Remember, you only have a measure of time and it must not be wasted. The good news is that you have the power to control the enemies of your time.

Thirty Minutes A Day Principle–30MaDP

You will need something to guide you, if you desire to let go of the weights that slow you down, in order to achieve your G–P–A. Knowing that you have lots of school work to do, you also need to know that it is unwise to leave other things that are of importance undone. These other things matter and they include spiritual activities (Bible study, praying, participation in your church activities…), family activities (house chores, working on projects, family time…), extracurricular activities (sports, skills, exercise…) and fun activities (games, movies, picnics, arts & crafts…).

- Spend at least 30 minutes praying and doing your personal Bible study. You can read A Chapter (of the Bible) A Day–ACAD and write in your journal what you learn.

- Spend 30 minutes a day reading inspirational books. Trying to finish reading in a day may not allow room for other things. You can ask your parents/guardian to sign you up for a book club. This will motivate you to read, as you will receive reminders from the group. You will also have the opportunity to share your insights from the book with others and learn from them as well.

- You might need to spend multiples of 30 minutes on your homework or study, depending on what you need to do. However, you can take a break after every 30 minutes, to use the restroom, have a drink, stretch, or snack, however, do not spend such a break on things that will steal your focus. Avoid piling up your homework and study as much as possible. Do not leave it to the last minute.

- Try to learn something new everyday (10 minutes) or every other day (20 minutes) or every three days (30 minutes).

- Take house chores seriously. See it as a service and learning opportunity. You may need to spend 30 minutes or less or even more but you should do as much as you are meant to do. You can speak to your parents politely to excuse you if you need to study more for your examinations or to prepare for something that is equally important.

- Spend 30 minutes or less to journal your activities for the week in order of priority and fit them into your timetable. Remember to also review your G–P–A for the previous week. You can use Sunday evenings to do that.

- Use 30 minutes or less every evening to review the passing day and plan the following day.

Note these also:

- Wake up early and do not sleep late, to be able to achieve your G–P–A in an excellent way.

- Limit the watching of TV to weekends, unless it is educational or part of your learning.

- Be accountable to someone you trust (your parent, sibling, mentor or a good friend).

Quick Reminder

T - Treasure it
I - I–must Guard it
M - Maximize it
E - Evaluate it

Fill It Out

Mention two new facts you learnt about time.

_____

_____

Which category do you belong—No time, less time or enough time?

_____

Mention three ways to gain more time.

_____

_____

_____

What are your time stealers and wasters?

_____

_____

_____

_____

In order of priority, write three things that are of importance that you need to start applying the 30MaDP to.

_____

_____

_____

A sample of a timetable you can fill up with your activities

	Mon.	Tue.	Wed.	Thur.	Fri	Sat.	Sun.
6–7am							
7–8am							
8–9am							
9–10am							
10–11am							
11am–12noon							
12–1pm							
1–2pm							
2–3pm							
3–4pm							
4–5pm							
5–6pm							
6–7pm							
7–8pm							
8–9pm							

TWO

Joseph's Friend

Just as lotions and fragrance give sensual delight,
a sweet friendship refreshes the soul

—Proverbs 27:9

Ten Facts About True Friends

1. True friends are a treasure.
2. True friends pull one another along to do what is right.
3. True friends are confidants.
4. True friends build one another up.
5. True friends work together to be productive.
6. True friends love and forgive at all times.
7. True friends accept honest criticisms and praises from one another.
8. True friends comfort one another.
9. True friends bear one another's burden.

10.   True friends celebrate one another's victory.

Who Are You?

To know the kind of friend to select, you need to first have an understanding of who you are, which is your identity. In her book, 'Eagle's Identity', Tomilola shared about 'who you are and who you are not.'

Here are seven things to know about yourself once you become a child of God. These will also give you a lasting friendship as you get to know that your perfection is in Christ and not in your friend.

1.   Your identity is in Christ
2.   Your worth is in Christ
3.   Your joy is in Christ
4.   Your confidence is in Christ
5.   Your hope is in Christ
6.   Your help is in Christ
7.   Your sufficiency is in Christ

It is not God's will for anyone to be alone or lonely. He has so much interest in friendship and that's why He puts everyone in a family first or under the guidance of a carer. From there, you start developing interest in making friends. You can find a friend in a member of your family and also outside your home. However, once you know who you are, the friend you choose should align with the facts about true friends.

Let's talk about the different types of friends. Someone says there are three types of friends, but this chapter will not be complete without adding one more.

1.   A friend who stays with you for a reason
2.   A friend who stays with you for a season
3.   A friend who stays with you for a lifetime
4.   A friend who stays with you forever

A Friend Who Stays With You For A Reason

This is someone who becomes your friend either because of what he can give you or what he can get from you. The Bible tells us a very interesting story in the Book of Genesis, Chapter 33, about a man named Laban and his nephew, Jacob.

> Laban saw that he was prosperous because Jacob was living in his house and he asked him not to leave soon. Jacob's uncle tricked him several times to make sure he stayed as long as he could make him stay. Laban had two daughters named Leah and Rachel. Jacob loved Rachel and wanted her to be his wife. First, Laban told Jacob to work for him for seven years so he could marry Rachel whom he loved. After seven years, he was deceived and given Leah instead of Rachel. Jacob was unhappy when he discovered, but he still loved Rachel

and would do anything possible to have her.

After a week of marriage to Leah, Rachel was given to Jacob on the agreement that he would serve Laban for another seven years. After spending fourteen years altogether in the house of Laban, Jacob told him he was ready to go back to his country with his wives. On hearing this, Laban was upset and planned another trick to hold him down. Jacob worked for Laban for another six years until God spoke to him to leave. This time he did not tell Laban. He left when Laban was not at home.

Laban was so upset when he heard Jacob had escaped with his wives and flock, that he chased him until he found him. He couldn't hurt Jacob because God told him not to do so.

The story is interesting, right! Laban was into the relationship because of what he could get from Jacob and not only that, he also maltreated Jacob for twenty years.

A Friend Who Stays With You For A Season

We can apply the four seasons of nature to friendship. So, we have four seasons of friendship. The winter and fall seasons are unfriendly while the summer and spring are the friendly seasons. Not all seasonal friends are unfriendly, just the way winter and fall seasons have the purpose they serve. Seasonal friends can stay with you for months or years not only because of what they can give or get but also for mutual benefits.

- Seasonal friends could be in your life for a specific period, to make a positive impact. Once they complete their mission, they leave.
- Some come like Laban, as you earlier read.
- And some come, hang around for a while and leave when you have nothing else to offer them any longer, but you can't blame them. An example is Orpah. The story of Orpah can be found in the Bible, Ruth Chapter 2.

> There once lived a family of four in Bethlehem; a couple and their two sons. The man's name was Elimelech, the woman was called Naomi and the sons were named Mahlon and Chillion. They relocated to Moab when there was famine in Bethlehem. They lived happily in Moab and all of a sudden, death struck and took away Elimelech. Not so long after, Mahlon and Chilion got married to Moabite ladies. Mahlon's wife was named Ruth while Chilion's was Orpah. Again, their happiness turned into bitterness. The unimaginable happened; death struck and snatched the two sons away one after the other.

Naomi, having lost almost everything, decided to go back to her country. Since the ladies were Moabites, she told Orpah and Ruth to go back to their families. Orpah left after some persuasion. Why? She must have thought staying with Naomi for the rest of her life might not bring her any good, afterall she had no son left to be married to.

Orpah and Naomi stayed together as long as the two of them had something to offer but shortly after they discovered there was nothing more to offer each other in the relationship, the two of them separated peacefully. This does not make Orpah a bad friend but that was the last time Orpah was mentioned in the Bible.

A Friend Who Stays With You For A Lifetime

This is the friend to be cherished as long as you live. They fit into the facts about true friends. Just like you, they have their imperfections and struggles but their value cannot be measured.

Examples of good friends in the Bible are: David and Jonathan, Paul and Timothy, Naomi and Ruth, Daniel, Shadrach, Meshach and Abednego and several others. All these people were there for one another for a lifetime.

We are sure you have been wondering, "The examples of

friendship mentioned in all the stories above are from the Bible. What about in this present age? Can we really find true friends?" Yes we can! Let's look at a true life story of two friends–Ken and Francis.

> Ken and Francis were six and eight years old respectively, when they met for the first time at a soccer club. As time went on, they discovered that they had similar values. They got to know each other's house and family and they turned out to be best of friends that were inseparable. They got admission into the same high school. They did virtually everything together; they looked out for each other, shopped together, spoke up for each other, trusted each other, accepted each other's imperfections, celebrated each other and above all prayed together. Does this mean they did not quarrel or have moments of disagreement? They did. But they understood that no one is perfect. Unfortunately, the duo couldn't get admission into the same university, but they promised each other to keep their friendship, no matter the distance. Even though they were apart, they kept building themselves up, with prayer and words of encouragement. Discussion about fulfilling their purpose and becoming the light of the world was not left out.

At the time of writing this book, Ken and Francis are married to lovely wives with children. They are still friends, they share ideas from parenting, business, investment, to impacting lives. They have achieved so many things together, and God is using them to help others restore and build good relationships.

To be a Joseph, the pride of Nations, God wants you to build a healthy lifetime relationship that He can use to transform other relationships. You need someone who can stay with you through thorns and roses and who you are also ready to stay with through times of challenges and celebrations. True friends guide and support one another to become the persons they were created to be.

A Friend Who Stays With You Forever

A man of many companions may come to ruin, but there is a friend who sticks closer than a brother.
—Proverbs 18:24

This is the friend who never calls it quits with you even if all other friendships fail. You may not be able to settle in any relationship until you settle with Him. He is the Ultimate Source where lifetime friends draw wisdom, inspiration and help from.

"There is a friend who sticks closer than a brother." His name is Jesus. He is the only BFF–Best Friend Forever, here on earth and in heaven. He stays with you even if your lifetime friend turns his back against you. There is no friend like Him. Becoming a friend of Jesus is the greatest choice you are encouraged to make. He will show and guide you on the right path to enjoy the best in this life, how to become one of the greatest leaders, and also give you access into God's family here on earth and the eternal home–Heaven, where you get to see the Father face to face.

The friend that comes into your life for a reason cannot give you this permit. Your seasonal friend does not have the key either. Your lifetime friend (like other friends) can only lead you to Jesus, but he cannot grant you access into God's family. Only Jesus can.

> *Jesus answered, "I am the Way and the Truth and the Life. No one comes to the Father except through Me"*
>
> *–John 14:16*

How Can You Then Make Jesus Your BFF?

Are you yet to make Jesus your BFF? Or was He once your BFF? Are you ready to make Him your BFF again? Take a pause, put your hand on your chest and then pray this prayer of salvation…

Father, I thank You for loving me,
I believe You sent Your only Son, Jesus to die for
me and to wipe my sins away,
I throw away all the sins I have committed,
I say bye bye to all the bad things I used to do,
Forgive me Jesus,
I invite you into my heart,
Come into my heart to stay,
Help me live to please You all the days of my life,
Help me to grow daily like You,
Help me to remain steadfast in You.
In Jesus name I pray. Amen.

Congratulations! You are welcome into God's family. Write today's date down in your special book or diary, and title it, *"The day I gave my life to Christ."* This is an important date to remember all the days of your life. It is worth celebrating every year as long as you are on the Lord's side.

You need to know that the devil would try to draw you back to the bad things you have thrown away, he might even tell you that you are not a child of God. Whenever you think you are hearing such a voice, tell him, 'I am no more a sinner, I am no more a slave to sin, I am free, I am a child of God.' Okay!

If you mistakenly do any bad thing, ask God, who is now your loving Father to forgive you and He will. God has become your Father and He loves you so much and does not want to lose you to sin again.

Seven Killers Of Friendship

A boy wonders, "I don't seem to settle in any relationship. None has ever worked out well." For your friendship to work, you need to avoid the following killers at all costs.

1. **Wrong Association**–Review your circle of friends and activities regularly. You don't have to continue with a friend that is leading you to do what is wrong, especially if he refuses to turn a new leaf. *"Don't fool yourselves. Bad friends will destroy you."–1 Corinthians 15:33*

2. **Comparison**–When you start comparing yourself with your friend or your ability with his', you are in the process of killing your relationship. The only person you should compare yourself with is YOU–the pride of Nations that God wants you to become. *"Pay careful attention to your own work, for then you will get the satisfaction of a job well done, and you won't need to compare yourself to anyone else."–Galatians 6:4*

3. **Envy and Jealousy**–In Chapter 9, you will see what this pair does and tips on how you can stay out of it. *"I have also learned why people work so hard to succeed: it is because they envy the things their neighbors have. But it is useless. It is like chasing the wind."–Ecclesiastes 4:4*

4. **Gossipping**–Avoid telling others about your friend's weaknesses or secrets. *"A troublemaker plants seeds of strife; gossip separates the best of friends."–Proverbs 16:28*

5. **Malice**–This is a feeling of hatred, grudge or bitterness against someone. It could be as a result of someone being unkind to you or you could even be the one

envious or jealous of your friend. Once this feeling appears, avoid feeding or nursing it, so it doesn't overpower you. *"So put away all malice and all deceit and hypocrisy and envy and all slander."–1 Peter 2:1*

6. **Unkindness**–Unkindness is an act of keeping things that will benefit or save your friend to yourself, and this includes information amid other things. *"He who withholds kindness from a friend forsakes the fear of the Almighty."–Job 6:14*

7. **Unhealthy Competition**–A Joseph doesn't engage in competition with the motive to outrun his friend. He would rather help his friends and see them succeed. One of the well–known writers, Harold Kushner says, *"When you come to look back on all that you have done in life, you will get more satisfaction from the pleasure you have brought into other people's lives than you will from the times that you outdid and defeated them."*

F – Finding a true friend is searching for a treasure

R – Review your circle of friends regularly

I – Identity of a true friend is in Christ

E – Envy ruins friendship

D – Darling Jesus is the only BFF

Fill It Out

State three differences between the best friend forever (BFF) and other friends.

_____

_____

_____

_____

Mention five friendship killers.

_____

_____

_____

_____

What does the Bible say about each of the killers?

_____

_____

_____

_____

_____

In what category can you place your friendship? *E. G. Lifetime...*

_____

_____

State three things you can start doing daily to improve your friendship.

_____

_____

_____

_____

_____

_____

_____

THREE

Joseph's Gratitude

I will give thanks to You, LORD, with all my heart; I will tell of all Your wonderful deeds.
—Psalm 9:1

Ten Facts About Gratitude

1. Gratitude is a treasure.
2. Gratitude is being thankful.
3. Gratitude is the best attitude.
4. Gratitude empowers God.
5. Gratitude boosts your self—esteem.
6. Gratitude connects you to helpers.
7. Gratitude enhances your relationships.
8. Gratitude motivates you to be more thankful.
9. Gratitude is a choice you make.
10. Gratitude is a journey.

Attitude

Gratitude has a lot to do with attitude and it will be good to understand what ATTITUDE means.

'Attitude' as described by Winston Churchill, "is a little thing that makes a big difference."

Attitude simply means the way one feels about something or someone which is caused by behaviour.

Attitude could be good or bad and it is shaped by some factors. Let's look at some of these factors:

- **Family:** The family in which you were born or raised has a lot of impact on the person you are becoming. Why? This is your foundation, the early formation stage. Your attitude could be as a result of what you see your parents or siblings do (either right or wrong) and you start acting it out, consciously or unconsciously.

- **Society:** Your society includes your school, community, country, clubs, place of worship and other places you go to. This also has a great impact on you because you tend to pick from the culture of where you are and also see things the way society sees it.

- **Association:** This talks about your relationships especially with your peers and other people you come across in your journey through life. You can read *Chapter 2* again to refresh your memory about friendship.

- **Ability (or Talent, Skill, Gift):** All these go hand in hand. It is very important we talk about ability. While some boys have allowed their talents to affect their attitude positively, some have allowed pride to take over them and it has had a negative impact on their attitude.

- **Thoughts:** What you think about has a greater impact on your attitude. For example, if you have limiting beliefs about yourself, it's going to affect your self–worth negatively, however if you have positive beliefs about yourself, it will have a positive impact on your attitude.

Do you aspire to become the Joseph God has created to lead, wherever he finds himself? One thing you need to know, before you read on, is that attitude is a journey. The earlier you choose the right attitude and you start nurturing it, the better.

The Attitude Of A Transformed Leper

The Bible tells us an interesting story about ten lepers in *Luke 17:11–19*. Let's read through:

> Now on his way to Jerusalem, Jesus travelled along the border between Samaria and Galilee.

As he was going into a village, ten men who had leprosy met him. They stood at a distance and called out in a loud voice, "Jesus, Master, have pity on us!"

When he saw them, he said, "Go, show yourselves to the priests." And as they went, they were cleansed.

One of them, when he saw he was healed, came back, praising God in a loud voice. He threw himself at Jesus' feet and thanked him and he was a Samaritan.

Jesus asked, "Were not all ten cleansed? Where are the other nine? Has no one returned to give praise to God except this foreigner?" Then he said to him, "Rise and go; your faith has made you well."

The Attitude Of A Joseph

You are never too young to lead wherever you find yourself. The story of Joseph in the Bible affirms it and you will read about it in the last chapter of this book. The attitude God wants you to develop is the right attitude. There are many people who lead but only few are purposeful leaders. Here are **TEN** life and leadership lessons we can draw from the attitude of a transformed leper, a foreigner who returned to give praise to God.

1. A Joseph must have faith in God.
2. A Joseph must show gratitude to God.
3. A Joseph must lead with the right attitude.
4. A Joseph must be willing to let go of the wrong way of life and learn the right way of life.
5. A Joseph must look beyond his culture, environment and his peers.
6. A Joseph must not allow anything to hold him back from doing what is right.
7. A Joseph must be humble.
8. A Joseph must live the life he leads.
9. A Joseph must not do things in order to draw attention to himself.
10. A Joseph must show gratitude to people for their acts of kindness.

Gratitude To God

"One of them, when he saw he was healed, came back, praising God in a loud voice."

What is your attitude when you give gratitude to God? We can see from the leper, when he saw that he was healed, he went back to Jesus and praised God in a loud voice. God is to be praised whether He does something for you or not. Develop the habit early in life to always thank God for being the Almighty. However, any time you experience the goodness of God, give Him the best gratitude.

Let's look at three things God is looking for in your Gratitude to Him:

1. **Purity:** How pure are your hands and heart, as a Joseph, the pride of Nations? *Only those whose hands and hearts are pure, who do not worship idols and never tell lies (can worship Him).–Psalm 24:4*

2. **Originality:** How genuine are you? Do you use your mouth to worship God and also use it to say things that do not glorify Him? *Through Jesus, therefore, let us continually offer to God a sacrifice of praise, the fruit of lips that openly profess his name.–Hebrews 13:15*

3. **Concentration:** How focused and consistent are you in knowing the way of God and living it out? *You will keep him in perfect peace, whose mind is stayed on You, because he trusts in You."–Isaiah 26:3*

When you give gratitude to God, worship Him by calling His beautiful names and thank Him for the privilege of having a relationship with Him. Always thank God for the specific things you enjoy or have; gift of life, sound health, your talents, every little and huge step you take towards your achievement and for everything, plus the things He is yet to do. Remember not to hide the gratitude you are meant to give God from Him and do not give the worship meant to Him to human beings, things or your abilities.

Gratitude To People

"He threw himself at Jesus' feet and thanked Him . . ."

What is your attitude when someone is being kind to you? The following will guide you to give the best gratitude.

- Never develop an entitlement mindset towards what people do for you.
- Do not take people's acts of kindness for granted.
- Go back to express your gratitude.
- Your gratitude can put a smile on the face of the person who shows you kindness.
- Show gratitude to anyone who is being kind to you regardless of their age.
- 'Thank you', 'I am sorry', 'Please', 'God bless you', and other compliments must come from your heart.
- Give human beings the gratitude meant to them and be careful not to turn them into gods.

Music, Lyrics and Dance–MLD

Gratitude can be expressed through music, lyrics or dance. The Joseph that will lead others to do the right thing must himself do the right thing. The content and type of your music, lyrics and dance matter a lot when expressing gratitude to God or people. The gratitude you render in the form of MLD is inspired by what you think, watch or listen to, and what you think, watch or listen to will be your choice. The way you would know if you have chosen the right or wrong MLD, is when it influences you to do the right or wrong thing respectively. You need to make up your mind to be a Joseph that will stand out in your generation, wherever you find yourself.

An extensive study took place to find someone who perfectly displayed the creativity of MLD–Music, Lyrics and Dance, to show gratitude to God. No other person qualified, except David.

David was known as a man of worship and a man of worship is known as a man of MLD. He wrote most of the chapters (Lyrics) in the book of Psalms, in songs (Music) to God. However, we will be talking about his Dance, which we call 'David's Dance'. We will share the story in a drama. However, we encourage you to read *2 Samuel 6:14–22*, for better understanding.

David's Dance

David, joyfully dancing to the Lord. (Sure he must have sweated till his garment got drenched…)

David: *(At home)* Hello, hi, sweetheart… Is someone at home?

Michal: *(Comes out angry)* David, David, David… What went wrong with you today?

David: What are you talking about?

Michal: *(Yelling)* Stop pretending

David: I don't understand

Michal: Have you forgotten the way you danced before the maids so soon?

David: Oh! Sweetheart, you meant dancing and rejoicing before the Lord about the arrival of our new wave of blessing?

Michal: No, I meant how you danced carelessly before the maids.

David: Dear, I couldn't express what God has done for us in Lyrics and Music only, but also with a dazzling Dance.

Michal: Did you just say a dazzling dance?

David: Yes dear, it was not to the maids but to the Lord and it was honorable to Him.

Michal: Rendered half–naked?

David: Dear, I wasn't lost in the dance to pull off my garment. The Spirit of God was so mighty upon me, but He didn't take off my garment either.

Michal: *(Still very upset, fixing her gaze on David)*

David: As long as I live, I will celebrate the Lord with more of this dazzling dance. I am not going to dance to the tune of the world but to the tune set by the Lord.

Will you stop expressing gratitude to God through MLD, because of what people think of you? Will you choose the world's design or God's? One day, you will become a great leader, do not allow your position or title to put a cap on your gratitude. Choose your MLD wisely and use it to glorify God, wholeheartedly.

The Bible verse below will guide you on how to choose your MLD:

> *"And now, dear brothers and sisters, one final thing. Fix your thoughts on what is true, and honorable, and right, and pure, and lovely, and admirable. Think about things that are excellent and worthy of praise."*
>
> *–Philippians 4:8.*

Make this Scripture your song, day and night and let it be your standard. Then you will be able to share the love of God and your value with your friends and others. You will also have the opportunity to lead them to Jesus Christ.

Remember, when we talk about MLD, David is the pick for us, and He can also be your model. It is so interesting to see how David became a light in the music world. You can become a leader right where you are; don't wait to get into the music industry before making a difference. The decision you make to stand for Jesus by the songs you choose to sing, listen or dance to may look awkward to your friends, but it is a giant decision to turn the hearts of many to God in the long run. And remember, whenever you are given the opportunity to plan an event or take the lead, ask God to direct you to select the music, lyrics and dance steps that will glorify Him.

Thank You Lyrics

The things you enjoy in life are not free. Even if you do not pay for them, know that someone paid or sacrificed something on your behalf. 'Thank you' goes a long way in expressing gratitude. You could also add a small gift or card to your lyrics (words). Below are some ways you can spice up your 'Thank you.'

- Thank you for guiding me to discover my purpose.
- Thank you for believing in me.
- Thank you for being a part of my success story.
- Thank you for motivating me.
- Thank you for being an inspiration.
- Thank you for your time, it means a lot to me.
- Thank you for sharing such wonderful information with me.
- Thank you for teaching me to become a godly man.
- Thank you for pulling me along to do the right thing.
- Thank you for your words of encouragement/affirmation.
- Thank you for the opportunity/gift.
- Thank you for leading me to Christ.

In conclusion, there is nothing you have unless God gives it to you or He asks someone to give it to you. However, being ungrateful can have a negative impact on your relationship with God and people. So choose the best attitude–GRATITUDE.

Quick Reminder

G – Grateful
R – Regularly
A – Attitude
T – Thankful heart
I – Immediately
T – Timely
U – Uplift
D – Donate
E – Express

Fill It Out

What is the best attitude?

_____

_____

_____

_____

What can you do differently to improve your gratitude to God?

_____

_____

_____

_____

Write down three names of people who have done amazing things for you and send them 'Thank you' lyrics. You can use the ones written in this book as a guide.

_____

_____

_____

_____

Review the songs you sing, listen or dance to and be true to yourself by answering this ONE question, based on Philippians 4:8... Are *they true, honorable, right, pure, lovely, admirable, excellent and worthy of praise?*

_____

_____

_____

State three things you can start doing to make a difference in your music world? Remember, the change starts with you.

_____

_____

_____

_____

_____

PART TWO

Joseph's Place In The Society

DISCOVERING OUR GOD–GIVEN PURPOSE IS never easy. Even more difficult is identifying who you are, and how your personality fits perfectly into God's plan.

Many people sometimes get it all wrong and desire some gifts that would not propel them to higher heights. Some know that every gift is given by God, but they encounter a challenge–how to continuously yield to God as His good representatives on earth. Others know their gifts, how they fit perfectly in God's plan and that they have to be His representatives 24/7. But again, there could be something lacking; the zeal to carry on when things get tough and the strength to sail through God's plans and purposes.

This section of this book would teach you exactly how to discover yourself, your God–given potential and how it all fits into the bigger picture—the purpose of God for your life. It would also teach how to position yourself as a good and faithful ambassador of God wherever you find yourself. And it will equip you with the right mindset you need to have to draw strength from God each day to go about your duties.

In this section, we will be discussing:
4.   Potential to Purpose
5.   I am an Ambassador
6.   My Ultimate Source of Strength

CHAPTER FOUR

Potential To Purpose

WHO SAYS YOU CANNOT BE all that God says you will be? Who says you are not worthy of leading a great impact? Who says that you cannot be the great person that God wants you to be, because of your insecurities? Do people's opinions about your future matter at all? Does what I think about myself, both the good and bad, even matter? Or there must be a final word declared and spoken over me that matters regardless?

He Doubted

Above are some of the questions that most people have to answer as they journey through life.

There was a talented young gentleman who looked down on himself so much and thought that nothing good could come out of his life. He lived in a community filled with young people who were doing great things, like owning small businesses as teenagers. He really struggled to hold up the little club he had running in school. The patrons of the club at school always looked down on his leadership abilities. Why? Because they thought that if only he led their way, then he would be a successful leader. And since he thought differently, he was not quite the fit for them. With time, he lost confidence in his leadership abilities and thought that he would become like every other person who lived a very quiet life of no impact to the world. He began to care less about leadership, and stepped down from leading the club. He moved from one happy child to a very sulky boy, with so much hurt, pain and disbelief, because of what his club patrons had told him.

Many children are easily let down by the words of others who do not know them and who do not understand their makeup. But for the One who made them, they found it so hard to believe His Word concerning their lives. Maybe because they cannot see the One, or maybe because they think all of those great things seem far because of their present circumstances.

From Doubter to Believer

The story of Moses in the Bible, the chosen leader of God comes to mind. Moses was a doubter, a doubter of not only his abilities, but also a doubter of what God had said concerning his life. God had ordained him to be a priest to His people, the Israelites. But he stuttered really bad, and so he thought he was not a good fit; he thought he was not a potential. It took God showing him what to say and giving him various signs to prove to him that he was chosen, regardless of his inadequacies.

> *Indeed, when God said he uses the foolish things of this world to shame the wise (1 Corinthians 1:27), He really meant it.*

So, Whose Opinion Matters?

After harbouring the feeling of being inadequate to lead for some time, it began to tell on him and how he approached issues at school. His grades began to slump. He was no longer interested in extracurricular activities. He just decided to live a life that had no positive impact on the next person. Then one day, he stumbled on this Bible verse that changed his life forever.

> *"I knew you before I formed you in your mother's womb. Before you were born I set you apart and*

appointed you as my prophet to the nations"
–Jeremiah 1:5

This verse hit him differently. Why? Because it rekindled the hope he had within him that he was capable, and he too had a potential, just like all the other boys in his community. He read about Jeremiah's story and saw how he thought he was inadequate, because he was young and thought he could not speak for nations to hear. He saw God's Word to him and realised that even a person's opinion did not matter. Rather, it is only the Creator's opinion that mattered.

Potential: A capacity within, yet to manifest or showing early signs of manifestation.

"So, what happens if the potential I think I have is not what God says I should focus on?", he began to think to himself.

Sometimes, what you think may be your potential may not be what God wants you to focus on. When you follow your own lead, outside of the will of God, it might start out well, but would still feel inadequate when others start to talk you down.

He was determined to know whether what he was thinking was true. He rushed to his father immediately and poured his heart out to him. Then it all made sense to him when his father explained to him.

Many times, people think they are better suited at something, because of their abilities. Moses probably thought he was going to stay in the wilderness all his life, after running away from being caught for killing someone in Egypt. Jeremiah might have thought that he was meant to stay at home and live a quiet life. But God who created them, spoke a Word from the beginning and it came to pass in their lives; He just needed to align them to that path.

How Do I Align to God's Plan for Me?

"There should certainly be a way to know where my true strength is, so I live out a life of impact", he said.

Yes! There is a way, and that way is to discover God's purpose for your life.

God's Purpose and My Potential

Purpose: An outcome that has been determined long before it is lived.

Rick Warren, in one of his books, discussed a practical way of identifying our purpose and potential in life using S–H–A–P–E.

But before we move on, we have to understand why it is

When we discover God's purpose for our lives, handling people's ideas about us and our potential becomes easy. We listen to them but do not act on their opinions unless they are true.

necessary to find our purpose in life.

Why Do I Need to Find My Purpose?

When you live a life of purpose:
- You will live a life of impact.
- You will be able to identify the distractions on your way and avoid them.
- You will not take the words of those who want to talk you down to heart. This is because, you will know who God says you are and determine to walk in it.
- The lines will fall for you in pleasant places (Psalm 16:6)–as you go about the work the Master has given you, He will bless you immeasurably.
- You will live a life of fulfilment and happiness. Many people achieve so much with a potential but are never happy. Those who are careful to live out their purpose find this inner peace, joy and happiness that can never be explained.

Get Your S–H–A–P–E On!

Have you ever wondered why it is very difficult to fit yourself into that pair of trousers you want to wear? Well, your guess is as good as ours! You are not putting on your correct size of trousers.

Think about your potential and purpose this way. You need to get your potential in S–H–A–P–E, aligned with God's purpose for Your life, so you bear much fruit and live a life of happiness. So, let's go through all the letters of S–H–A–P–E in detail.

S - Spiritual Gift(s)

Before God created us, He placed his special gifts in us, as a seal to show us where we are to function in life for Him. Just like the way all your fingers are not equal, God did not create us with equal gifts. But it does not mean that if someone has a particular gift, the person is better than you.

> *"A spiritual gift is given to each of us so we can help each other"*
> *–1 Corinthians 12:7*

And once we know what our spiritual gift is, we will know where to function, and we will find fulfilment once we operate in it. According to 1 Corinthians 12, there are many spiritual gifts:

- **Apostolic gift:** A gift that enables one to inspire and influence other people to live right, like Apostle Paul in the Bible.
- **Prophetic gift:** A gift that enables someone to see into the future, like Joseph and Prophet Jeremiah in the Bible.
- **Teaching gift:** A gift that enables a person to tell others exactly how they are to go about a situation, like Philip in the New Testament, who explained to the Ethiopian

eunuch what he was reading from God's Word.

- **The gift of working miracles:** A gift that causes impossible situations to be possible.
- **The gift of healing:** A gift that enables a person to help others get healed from their diseases, through their great faith, like Prophet Elisha to Naaman.
- **The gift of helping others:** A gift that enables a person to be of great help to others, like Mary and Martha in the Bible.
- **The gift of leadership:** A gift that enables a person to lead others unto the right path that leads to life and goodness, like Moses.
- **The gift of speaking to God in an unknown language:** A gift that makes one communicate with God in a very special way, like those who speak in unknown tongues when praying.
- **The gift of interpreting dreams, Godly languages, and tongues:** A gift that makes one help others understand mysteries so everyone is edified, like Joseph in the Bible, who had the rare gift of interpreting dreams and mysteries.

It is also interesting to note that though God gives everyone a spiritual gift or more according to their purpose on earth, spiritual gifts can also be desired and prayed for. God will give that gift to the one who desires, after He has evaluated the motive behind the request and found that it is not for selfish gain, but to benefit people.

H–Heartfelt Passion(s)

Sometimes, you might wake up with a strong burden on your heart to change the fact that people do not dispose of waste appropriately. Whenever you are walking to school and come across a child who is homeless, something kicks inside of you to want to change the fate of that child at all costs. Whatever makes you want to change a situation so badly, is most likely a heartfelt passion. Heartfelt passions are sometimes an indicator of what God wants us to focus on. Out of it, we discover our unique potentials that would help us achieve these desires in our heart.

A–Abilities

Ability: The quality of being able to perform something, naturally. It is sometimes referred to as a skill or talent.

Do you sing with ease? When you put pen to paper, is it very easy for you to organise your thoughts? Do you find yourself tapping your feet and moving your body at the least sound of music? Is it very easy for you to write good lyrics to a beat without planning? Whatever you find easy to do, most likely is an ability. It is very possible that one person would have more than one ability. Why? Because human beings are very complex and grand in a very beautiful way. Humans are very powerful beings with many capabilities.

P–Personality

Personality: Unique characteristics of a person's behaviour that define a person.

According to Myers–Briggs, there are a summary of eight (8) personality types that define a person. The interesting thing about these personality classifications is that one person could have more than one of these traits. The personality types are displayed in the next table.

Quadrant 1

Extroverts

They are very energetic and love to do so many things at a time. Some of them like to go about their duties in a fast manner and they thrive in busy environments.

Introverts

They prefer to work alone or with a few people. Vibrant and energetic environments take their energy away, literally. They prefer to focus when working at something and do not mind taking their time to do what has to be done well.

Sensors

They are realistic and like to focus on the truth and facts about any situation they are in. They draw lots of inspiration from their past experiences. Therefore, they are seen to apply 'common sense' most times. Hence, their solutions to issues are very practical and relatable.

Intuitives

They easily detect patterns in whatever they do. Such people would find verbal reasoning and series and sequence (under Mathematics) pretty easy. They focus on what is possible under every situation and would like to know what the future holds.

Quadrant 3

Quadrant 2

Thinkers

They make decisions using logical analysis. This means that they would have to be very honest with themselves about the facts of a situation, so they are able to outline the good and bad outcomes in a scenario, in order to decide what to do. They like to be with people who tell them the truth and are fair and consistent in their words and actions.

Feelers

They are very sensitive. As such, other people who are not like them must be careful how they treat and talk to them because they try to read the hidden meaning behind most actions and words. Whatever they are able to accept and tolerate must reflect their values and what they treasure.

Judgers

They are very organised and prepared for almost every situation. As such, they cannot understand why some people could be unprepared sometimes. Also, they like to stick to plans and routines (timetables) because it makes them organised. Such people find it very easy following rules and a structure.

Perceivers

They are able to act in a very spontaneous manner. For them, anything goes, once it makes sense and they go with the best option at a particular time. As such, they would prefer not to plan things.

Quadrant 4

E–Experience(s)

Have you ever gone through a situation that defined your thinking on how to handle a particular circumstance? Did you ever decide to do something based on what happened to you or someone else some time back? Well, you are using your experience to decide what you will do. Experiences sometimes serve as a guide in helping us discover what we are comfortable with, and what we can do. Sometimes, experiences may not exactly help us in discovering ourselves, especially when they are not personal experiences. As such, experiences are like the wind–it helps you fly at some point and sometimes it does not (that is when it blows in the opposite direction). That is why you need to know which experience you consider important in understanding your personality.

Potential Turned Purpose

> Jacob was the younger of the twins God blessed Isaac and Rebekah with. Ordinarily, his elder twin brother Esau, should have been the heir to their father's inheritance. But God chose Jacob to receive all the blessings of a first child, according to His special plan for his life. He spent 20 years working for his uncle Laban, after fleeing his father's house with what everyone would have thought was Esau's blessings.

Though he had a difficult time working with his uncle, God gave him the *ability to literally turn dust to beautiful gold bars.* The Bible records that when Jacob worked under his uncle, God blessed him immeasurably. His uncle had nothing to worry about concerning his wealth because Jacob was a natural wealth maker. He even created wealth for himself while working for his uncle, by taking over the spotted animals that his uncle did not want in his fold.

God gave him a *perceiver's personality*, and this made it easy for God to direct and talk to Him. He recognised God in many ways, and once God spoke to him, there was no way he ever resisted it because that personality trait made him always ready to act in a spontaneous and sensitive manner towards God. To Jacob, he always knew that God's way was the best there could possibly be. Though he had a bad habit of tricking and lying to people, God did something wonderful.

Jacob had an *experience with God at Peniel* that changed the course of his life forever. He wrestled with God and lost. But the outcome of that experience and encounter was amazing. His name was changed to Israel. The trickster in him was taken away and replaced with God's desired nature for him. It was blessings and onward movement from then.

Our S–H–A–P–E adds up to the beautiful picture that God has for us, and the purpose He wants to use us for.

Quick Reminder

P – Prayerful
U – Unstoppable
R – Resilient
P – Planner
O – Optimistic
S – Self–disciplined
E – Enthusiastic

Fill It Out

Identify your S–H–A–P–E:

S–Spiritual Gift(s)

_____

_____

_____

_____

H–Heartfelt Passion(s)

_____

_____

_____

_____

A–Abilities

_____

_____

_____

_____

P–Personality

_____

_____

_____

_____

E–Experience(s)

_____

_____

_____

_____

_____

CHAPTER FIVE

I Am An Ambassador

IMAGINE BEING THE UNITED NATIONS (UN) Ambassador to a country. How do you think you would portray yourself at functions you have to represent the UN at?

Ambassador: Someone who has been ordered to act on another's behalf

Being a gentleman, you would want to look the best in every way. Aside from the fact that you may do well to look as good as every prim and proper person would, you may also do well to present yourself appropriately, like an ambassador, especially in deed and conduct. In summary, you may do either or all of the following:

- Speak and act like a leader and ambassador.
- Represent the UN well at all functions.

- If you have to try to fit in and make the people in your target country feel you as one of them, you probably will dress like the gentlemen in the country you are an ambassador at, but in a decent manner.

Basically, the above is what being an ambassador is. But sometimes, we see that not all people are good ambassadors, like the way you would behave in the scenario above. So, who then is a bad ambassador?

A Bad Ambassador

Let's take the story of Jonah in the Bible.

> Jonah was sent by God to preach the message of His salvation to the people of Nineveh, so they would repent. But he had other plans and thought the work was too much for him. He decided to run away from God and the work that had been assigned to him.

Imagine, as an ambassador, you are running from the one who has paid you and sent you to represent him/her well. That simply would just show the one who sent you that you do not believe all that they are telling you to do is possible. Or basically, you may just be saying, 'I am not bothered. I want to live my life without affecting the lives of others positively.' The truth of the matter is that one way to live a life of impact is to be an ambassador in all we do, and a good ambassador at that.

The story of Jonah reminds us of Proverbs 13:17.

> *An unreliable messenger stumbles into trouble, but*
> *a reliable messenger brings healing.*

Jonah became an unreliable messenger and ended in trouble when he was thrown over into the sea because of the huge storm that arose due to his running away. That is why, as we become ambassadors, we should be very careful we are good ambassadors.

What do Bad Ambassadors Do?

- They have other plans (bad plans) other than the reason they are sent.
- They do not care about the task they are sent to do.
- They act in an irresponsible manner.
- They eventually become a bad example to others.

The Big Question: Do you think that God calls some people to be bad ambassadors?

Well, your answer is as good as ours! Why would God call someone to act in a bad and irresponsible manner?

So, if God does not want us to be bad ambassadors, why does God need us to be good ambassadors?

Why Does God Need Us to be Good Ambassadors?

Because the world would be lost without good ambassadors. Good ambassadors are necessary to show the world the way it should go. That is why God asks us to be two things according to Matthew 5:13–14.

- **The salt of the earth**–to give the earth flavour because the attitudes of many people have caused it to have so much bitterness.

- **The light of the world**–because the attitudes of many people have caused the world to be filled with gloom, sorrow, and darkness.

You Are Called to be A Good Ambassador

Yes! Believe it or not, God has called you to be a good ambassador. It does not mean that you have to belong to a special organisation, like Elegant Initiatives, that will charge you to go out to serve and be of meaningful impact. What it means is, even in your room corner at home, you can be the ambassador that God has called you to be. Even as the only tall boy or short boy in your class, you can be the ambassador that God has called you to be. It starts with realising the ways that God has called you to be an ambassador.

And in case you may be wondering why you have to be an

ambassador for God (or Christ), read *2 Corinthians 5:20* below.

So, we are Christ's ambassadors; God is making His appeal through us. We speak for Christ when we plead, "Come back to God!"

The 3-Way Street to Ambassadorship

It is a simple 3-way street that begins and ends with God.

1.   Ambassador in Personality
2.   Ambassador in Society
3.   Ambassador for God and His Word

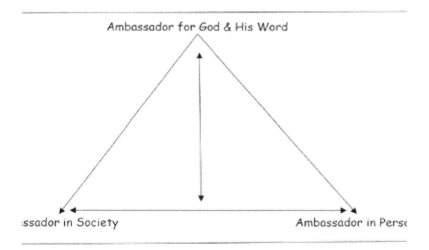

Ambassador in Personality

Do you remember the various personality types we looked at in the previous chapter? The table on the types of personality is a very useful guide to understanding people. You can go over it again, so you know who you are, understand people better and start learning to live and win with them.

And in learning to live with people, we must also understand that we have to portray good manners, characters, and personality, so that people will see your deeds and want to be like you and ultimately, like God.

> *In the same way, let your good deeds shine out for all to see, so that everyone will praise your heavenly Father*
> *—Matthew 5:16*

Being an ambassador of personality therefore means that you exhibit good behaviour in your conduct and relation with people and society. It means that you decide not to lie, when you think that is a way out, because you know that God is watching. It means that you give people good advice on not cheating in examinations and being that good example yourself when you are in an exam setting. It means living up to the good character traits that God has outlined in the Scripture to make Him proud that He has you as a representative on earth.

When you are an ambassador in personality:

- You do it for yourself, so that you will be blameless in the sight of God.
- You do it because truly, it is the right thing to do.
- You do it because you cannot afford to lead others unto the wrong path that leads to eternal condemnation.
- You do it because God is counting on you to do so and would be super proud of you if you did.

Ambassador in Society

Being an ambassador in society, now goes beyond your immediate surroundings and how your personality affects those close to you. God is counting on the good personality you have to change the society you are in. No wonder the Pinkie finger in the Elegant Initiatives Vision is so clear:

> *"Raising global ambassadors (in our communities and wherever we find ourselves)"*

You do not have a changed personality just to have it shelved in your room at home. You have a changed personality to share with your community and country at large. A boy reading this right now might be thinking this is far–fetched. But we can say for a fact that it is not.

Joseph and Daniel Company started with a few boys (not even up to ten) at the height of the COVID–19 pandemic. Lives were impacted from the beginning, even though many people did not know about it. With time, people started to partner to move the vision further and it is growing into a global movement.

Being an ambassador in society starts with a desire to change something. Once you start to take baby steps, like tidying your environment when it is dirty or giving to the less privileged items worth ten dollars or any amount, God will definitely look on your selfless desire and cause many good people to come your way to push the vision and desire you have very far. God will make it go as far as He wants it to go.

Ambassador for God & His Word

This must be the hardest part for most young people. And why is that? It is because to be an ambassador in God entails a lot of studying the Bible and waiting on Him in prayer in order to be empowered to proclaim His message without fail.

It is not enough to be of positive influence in society. Positive influence in society, which is not backed by the Word of God and His message of Redemption to humanity would lose its relevance with time. Have you ever seen very beautiful and lovely philanthropic works by great individuals that have lost value immediately the individual passes on to glory? You must have seen a number of them. You must have also seen great organisations that started many generations before the current vision bearers, that are still thriving. What do you think might be the difference? A hidden power, right?

Yes! And for you as a pride of Nations, that hidden power to back your move for societal change is the Word of God and your ability to constantly preach it. The preaching does not have to be the usual way your pastor does it at church. At Elegant Initiatives, all the children and individuals there can testify that the Word of God is preached in very fun ways. In fact, for every societal change that is embarked on at Elegant Initiatives, the team is sure to establish and maintain all the valuable faith–based messages that should back it. That is why the team always has to spend time reading, studying the Bible, and praying to be able to know what God has to say about every project.

Can you imagine what could possibly happen when you share the Word of God with the society?

- Many people who have not heard about Jesus Christ will get to know Him.
- Some people will have the opportunity to be saved unto the right path.
- They will live their lives pleasing God and they will also lead many other lost people unto God.
- The benefits that you as an ambassador will get for this move will be so much that you would not even have enough room to contain it.

The seeds of good deeds become a tree of life, and those who win souls are wise

—Proverbs 11:30

When you spread God's Word even as you carry on societal projects of change, God is telling you that you are a wise person, from the verse above, and your personal testimony will be great, even as the society you are impacting becomes better.

Remember! There is no great societal change without the presence and Word of God!

The 3-way Cycle Simplified

When you are an Ambassador for God and His Word, you become an Ambassador in Personality because your attitude would start reflecting the attitude of God. This means that you only act the way God would have acted under any situation. Once you become an Ambassador in Personality, you shine your light and give flavour to your environment by your actions, thereby becoming an Ambassador in society. Many people would see you and want to be like you. Then the negative behaviours and happenings in society would reduce gradually because people would want to be the good you.

Also, once you are an Ambassador for God and His Word, you automatically become an ambassador in society. It is very possible to be an Ambassador in personality and society, without being an Ambassador for God and His Word. Being an Ambassador for God and His Word is the ultimate we must strive for. We cannot be that if we have not accepted Jesus Christ into our hearts as our LORD and Personal Saviour. If you are yet to accept Him and you would like to accept Him now, say the salvation prayer in Chapter 2.

An Ambassadorial Plan

But how are all these ways to being a Good Ambassador achievable? Well, there is something we call an Ambassadorial Plan.

The journey to being an ambassador does not end with only the ways you can be a good one. You need to have a plan, a plan of action, a strategy on how you can carry it right from start to end.

Maybe you want to be an ambassador in personality, and you realise that you have a bad attitude of telling lies just to get yourself out of a fix when you have not achieved what you have to do, within the time you said you would. Then your plan(s) could be:

- To determine to tell the truth, no matter the situation.

- To meet your deadlines and promises made, so you do not tell lies.

Much like every plan you can make, you need to commit them to the LORD in prayer. One way to do that is by dedicating a part of your prayer journal to your ambassadorial plans and praying one plan a day. God listens to prayers and gives answers once they are coming from a heart of sincerity.

Quick Reminder

A – Agent of Change
M – Motivated
B – Bold
A – Ambitious
S – Sociable
S – Selfless
A – Accountable
D – Dedicated
O – Organised
R – Responsible

Fill it Out

Why does God need us to be ambassadors?

_____

_____

_____

_____

What is an ambassadorial plan? And how can you list out
your ambassadorial plan and live by it?

_____

_____

_____

_____

What ambassador status should we ultimately strive for? And
how can you be that ambassador?

_____

_____

_____

_____

CHAPTER SIX

My Ultimate Source Of Strength

E RIC WAS SUCH A BUBBLY boy in high school. He loved everything about his family. Seeing them during his school breaks just gave him a renewed sense of energy to pursue all that he had planned for them during his short stay with them. It took a trip to the United Kingdom to pursue his university education for him to realise that all he was ever able to do (his abilities and capabilities) were largely dependent on his family being around and supporting him in all he did. Once they were not visibly around, he felt he had lost it all, with no strength or willingness to go after what he needed to do. He simply depended on others for strength and happiness.

> *Strength: A capacity that enables a person to be intense at a task or endure a situation.*

Where Does Your Strength Lie?

There are so many young people, who literally run on the strength–tanks of others. And once these people are not strong again, or around, they seem to be unmotivated to carry on.

Some people run on the strength–tanks of things that do not last. Some people run on the strength of their own capabilities, that if they grow tired, nothing happens again. But is that how God wants to refuel our strength? Refuelling on things or people who are here today and gone tomorrow?

Two Important Things God says About Strength

1. **By (human) strength shall no man prevail (1 Samuel 2:9):** Many people depend on their human strength to get through life's challenges and issues. But God makes it clear that it is not just human strength we require to get through life. So, what strength do we require to move with in life?

2. **The joy of the LORD, which is our strength (Nehemiah 8:10):** You may be wondering how this can be true. Well, there was a time in the Bible days when the people of God felt as though everything was coming down and there was really no strength to move on. But through God's promises to His people, which

Ezra read to them, the LORD instructed His people to draw strength from Him and in the gladness that He alone brings! This shows us something, that our strength should be found in the LORD.

Characteristics of Strength

- It is a character that manifests within before it comes out.
- It can be seen when certain actions are expressed. For example, if a gentleman is able to rise early and perform some of his important duties in time before going to school, that is an expression of strength.
- It can be thought of as a battery, or a tank. Once running low or empty, it has to be refilled.

What Type of Strength Can God Provide Us?

Like we have read, God is to be our Ultimate Source of strength. This means that for every kind of strength you desire, He has the ability and a rich store of strength to deliver to you. What are some of the strengths we can draw from God?

- Physical/Bodily strength
- Emotional/Mental strength
- Spiritual strength
- Any other kind of strength

Physical/Bodily Strength

This kind of strength is exhibited when we have energy to go about the activities that require it. Some of the natural ways to gain and preserve this strength are:

- By having enough sleep, especially at night. Research has shown that the average number of sleep hours per day for school age children is eight (8) hours. That way, they will be energised for the day's activities.

- By taking short naps in the afternoon.

- By conserving your energy through a routine. Football players, for instance, do not go all through the day training. That could be physically draining and tasking. Therefore, they have a routine of short but effective practice sessions in the morning, afternoon, and evening, so their energy is conserved.

But do you believe that God can also give a person physical strength? Samson in the Bible had exceptional physical strength because of his hair and it was God who made it so. Elijah in the Bible raced physically to catch up with the chariot of King Ahab? That was exceptional physical strength right there! For a man to run as fast as a number of horses in a chariot requires a lot of physical strength and stamina. The Bible says it in an even beautiful manner.

*Then the LORD gave special strength to Elijah.
He tucked his cloak into his belt and ran ahead of
Ahab's chariot all the way to the entrance of Jezreel*
–1 Kings 18:46

Emotional/Mental Strength

Sometimes, you might be going through a tough time that requires emotional strength. Emotional and mental strength can be likened to an inner strength. That is the strength you need to get your inner self going and energised for whatever situation you may have. Emotional and mental strength from God comes in the following ways:

- Comfort from sorrow
- Calmness when trouble is sighted.
- Inner push to persevere when situations get tough.
- Wisdom to handle the many attitudes and characters you meet on your life's journey.
- Positive assurance and expression under any situation.

One person who exhibited great emotional and mental strength in the Bible when faced with many adversities for preaching the gospel was Paul the Apostle. He was human like us, and there must have been times he felt like crying when he was going through so much physical pain and abuse. But God encouraged him with His Word and that was what kept him going.

Spiritual Strength

"I want to be able to wake up and pray before going to school...Midway through my Bible study, I get exhausted and lose interest. The nice stuff around just take my attention away from the Bible. Honestly, I feel so bad every single time and wish I could do better."

The above and many more are common statements by people who need the extra push to go after what would edify them. But they do not find it easy doing so. It could be that they may have resolved to read their Bibles and pray, set alarms to help them out with that, but still find it a challenge. It is because they are trying to do it by their own strength.

> *...no one will succeed by [physical/human] strength alone*
>
> *—1 Samuel 2:9*

Sometimes, we need that extra push, called spiritual strength, to help us achieve what God requires from us from the Word. How does spiritual strength manifest?

- It creates an awakening within a person (which usually comes from revelation).

- This revelation would push them to do the right things according to God's Word, like reading the Bible, waiting on the LORD through prayers, fasting, and other spiritually exciting things.

- The individual would then realise that they do not have to use their physical strength to do spiritual exercises. They will be emboldened to seek after God in a supernatural way.

Any Other Kind of Strength

Some people have strength–needs that may not be easily voiced or explained. Whenever you are in such a situation, go to the LORD and humbly request that He refuels you in an extraordinary way.

Why The Need to Fuel/Refuel Our Strength?

We do not have the same strength consistently all the days of our lives. Take your grand–dad for instance. He probably does not have the strength to run around and go on long marathons like you would be able to do now. That shows that his physical strength to do such tedious running duties has reduced. It does not mean that he cannot run any longer. It just means he will require a bit more effort at replenishing his strength to do what he could do at his age.

"Have you ever heard of it? Have you ever understood? The LORD is the everlasting God, the Creator of all the earth. He never grows weak or weary. No one can measure the depths of His understanding. He gives power to the weak and strength to the powerless. Even youths will become weak and tired, and young men will fall into exhaustion. But those who trust in the LORD will find new strength. They soar high on wings like eagles. They will run and not grow weary. They will walk and not faint."

–Isaiah 40:28–31

We can see from the above verses that:

- Everyone lacks strength (depending on what your strength–need is) at one point in time, even if they are young people.

- But the LORD never grows tired, weak, or out of strength. He is the ever–solid rock of strength.

- Hence, we need to refuel our strength from Him because He never runs out of it. Imagine Him to be your electric socket that helps you charge your phone to 100% when it has almost 0% battery life. When you think of Him that way, your problem is half–solved. Now, what is the other thing that you have to do?

Steps to Fuelling/Refuelling the Strength that God Gives?

1. Trust in the LORD that He is the One who has the strength of all.
2. Wait on Him to fill you with His strength.

How do you wait on Him? Through PRAYER. It is not enough to just think that God knows that you need strength. It goes beyond that. Remember that He said we should pray about all things (Philippians 4:6), and that includes strength. When you seek His strength in prayer, He sure will give it to you.

How Do We Know that God has Filled Us?

*   We begin to feel exceptional strength in our area of need.
*   We start to do the things for which we require strength from the LORD.
*   God also fills us with wisdom in order to know how to gain our strength and how to use it.

A young boy reading this book is going to be a great leader someday. Performing your leadership role would require a lot from you in all aspects of your life. One of them is your strength. Sometimes, you may not get the praises of people, physical strength, or any kind of strength–bank to get you going. However, remember that God is there to listen to you when you have a strength–need. He will listen to you and equip you for the task ahead.

Quick Reminder

S–Spend quality time with God
T–Take Bible study seriously
R–Relate with the Holy Spirit regularly
E–Engage in strength–building activities
N–Never look down on your strengths
G–Give your best always
T–Take time to rest
H–Healthy living is wealthy living

Fill it Out

Here's a GOD Strength–Bank. Take time daily to pray over your strength–need for the day. Once they are answered, tick off the boxes. You can create another strength–bank once this is filled up.

Tick	Day	Strength–Need	Activity I Need Strength For
	e.g., Sunday	Physical Strength	To perform cleaning duties after church
	Sunday		
	Monday		
	Tuesday		
	Wednesday		
	Thursday		
	Friday		
	Saturday		

PART THREE

Overcoming My Inadequacies

Pride goes before a fall.

–Proverbs 16:18

PRIDE GOES BEFORE A FALL, as it is always said. These other negative traits precede a fall and not achieving what God has planned for our lives: fear, doubt, anger, envy, and jealousy.

When you fear to move in the direction that God has called you to, due to past experiences, or you doubt God's Hand in your life, to make you who He has called you to be, you might feel like God is not with you especially when situations are not going in favour of your expectation.

Sometimes, this might lead promising young boys into envy and jealousy, especially when they see young people like themselves, who are flourishing in their fields of endeavour.

They may start to question God and even the capabilities of their fellow colleagues who are thriving. And in no time, pride and anger set in.

This shall never be your story. That is why after you have learnt to live your life according to purpose, we want you to take hold of these little foxes and make sure that you do not succumb to them as you are on your journey to becoming the pride of Nations.

In this section, we will be discussing:
7.   Fear and Doubt
8.   Pride and Anger
9.   Envy and Jealousy

SEVEN

Fear And Doubt

Fear: An awareness of something not going on as one would positively expect it to.
Doubt: To be uncertain about the outcome of something. Sometimes, it could lead to a lack of confidence and an absence of faith and belief in something.

He Was Anxious…

…anxious about tomorrow. Anxious that he would not eventually get through high school, and then college, and eventually become a trail–blazing 'Joseph' in society. Even if he made it to college, he was uncertain he would graduate because he thought he was academically poor based on his test scores in basic school. An influencing factor was the fact that he did not have examples of people around him who flourished regardless of their circumstances. His father did not complete high school.

Many boys nowadays have the same mentality. There is one fear, one doubt, that makes them lose out on some great opportunities in life.

Many boys doubt they are good enough, that they fear they will make a mockery of themselves if they put an entry into any societal engagement. They fear the opinions of people, that they do not want to be on the wrong side of people's opinions.

In summary, in our world today, many people take decisions out of fear and doubt. Indeed, fear and doubt are siblings. They tug along all the time.

She Scared Him

One person that went through a significant moment of fear and doubt in the Bible was Elijah. Jezebel went after him because of the miracle he performed on the mountain *(1 Kings 19)*. He feared because Jezebel spoke life–threatening words to him. When he got tired, obviously from running away and being afraid, he started to doubt his calling as a prophet and even wished he would let it all go.

But God had a better plan for him. He had a perfect solution:

- Food was brought to him by ravens regularly, to clear his doubt of being called and taken care of by God.

- Direction on his next steps, to take his fear of human beings away.

What This Pair Does To Us

Much like Elijah, fear and doubt makes the following happen to us:
- It makes us think in a negative way.
- It makes us take actions that we would ordinarily not have taken, like running away, avoiding people, or doing stuff so we are in the good books of people.
- It makes us lose our faith in God and His Mighty Power, because we are depending on natural and human occurrences to happen.
- It makes us lose out on the bright future that God has planned for us.
- It punishes us, according to *1 John 4:18 as shown below.*

> *"…because fear involves punishment"*

After seeing all these negative effects of fear and doubt, you are wondering why you entertain them, to even begin with, right? Sometimes, it may not exactly be your fault that you entertain them.

How We Entertain Fear and Doubt Unknowingly

Naysayers around us. These people have nothing positive to

say about any situation. Usually, this would happen when we entertain and share our vision, future, present plans and purpose with just anyone and people who are not trusted.

When we think we are just like the ordinary person, we take cues from the past experiences of these people, which could affect us negatively. What we have to remember is that all of our lives are different, and we each have different journeys to live out on earth.

When we do not entertain enough of the Word of God; enough to build our faith and help us conquer every fear and doubt and trust in God more.

The Cure

Truly, the cure of fear and doubt is the Word of God.

"When I am afraid,
I will trust in You
Trust in You,
I will trust in You
When I am afraid,
I will trust in You
For You are my Saviour
and my LORD"

Some parts of the song above were taken from *Psalm 56:3–4*, and it reminds us of a sure step to handle our fear and doubt–Trusting in God.

But how can we trust God when we do not know His Word towards us and what He says about fear and doubt?

Trust: To hold on to something or someone, as if nothing else matters, or as if they are our only hope.

The first step to trusting God when afraid is by knowing the Word of God.

What Does GOD Say About FEAR and DOUBT?

FEAR

Psalm 27:1	*The LORD is my light and my salvation—so why should I be **afraid**?* **God Says:** Once we have Jesus Christ as our LORD and Saviour, and the light that directs our path, we have a strong and firm assurance that takes all fear away.
Psalm 23:4	*Even when I walk through the darkest valley, I will not be **afraid**, for you are close beside me.* **God Says:** He is always close to His children. Therefore, they should never be afraid even when they go through the toughest of circumstances because He will guide them through.

Psalm 46:1–3	*God is our refuge and strength, always ready to help in times of trouble. So, we will not **fear** when the earthquakes come and the mountains crumble into the sea.* **God Says:** When we are afraid, we should run to Him because He is our refuge, strength, and strong tower, even through difficult circumstances.
Psalm 91:4–5	*He will cover you with His feathers. He will shelter you with His wings. His faithful promises are your armour and protection. **Do not be afraid** of the terrors of the night, nor the arrow that flies in the day.* **God Says:** His feathers and wings are warm enough to provide us a shelter from all evil. And His promises to us are 'Yes' and 'Amen' and they will surely come to pass. He promises to take care of us forever. Therefore, we should not be afraid of any circumstance, because He has it all under control.

2 Timothy 1:7	*For God has not given us the spirit of **fear** and timidity, but of power, love, and self–discipline.*
	God Says: He never gives us a spirit of negativity, and that includes fear. Therefore, we should never entertain it. By His plan, He wants us to be very bold. If you lack boldness, go to Him in prayer and He will give it to you.

DOUBT

Matthew 14:31	*Jesus immediately reached out and grabbed him (Peter from drowning). "You have so little **faith**," Jesus said. "Why did you **doubt** me?"*
	God Says: God does not want us to doubt Him in any way. He wants us to have a strong faith in His power, might and ability because He is bigger than every circumstance.

James 1:6	*But when you ask Him, be sure that your* ***faith*** *is in God alone. Do not* ***waver***, *for a person with divided* ***loyalty*** *is as unsettled as a wave of sea that is blown and tossed by the wind.*
	God Says: God wants us to trust Him and Him alone. When we trust Him partly, it is a sign of disloyalty to Him because He is the Only Person who has been loyal to us since birth. And it breaks His heart when we doubt His competence and kindness to humanity.
James 1:7	*Such people should not expect to* ***receive anything from the LORD.***
	God Says: When we doubt and show signs of disloyalty, God says we do not receive anything from Him, and that includes answered prayers.

James 1:8	*Their **loyalty** is divided between God and the world, and they are unstable in everything they do.* **God Says:** When we doubt Him, it shows that we trust the world. The world is very unstable, and we become what we trust. So, we become unstable, like the world, and we blow around just like the wind, not knowing which direction we are headed.
Matthew 21:21	*Then Jesus told them, "I tell you the truth, if you have **faith** and do not **doubt**, you can do things like this and much more. You can even say to this mountain, 'May you be lifted up and thrown into the sea,' and it will happen".* **God Says:** Faith is as strong as anything you can imagine. It can make you do the impossible, God being your help. The solution you need is found in having faith in God.

You see you are missing out on key knowledge on fear and doubt, that could help you overcome them and grant you wisdom to apply them as a cure?

Steps To Applying The Cure

1.   Read the WORD everyday. You can start with stories

in the Bible of how people have been triumphant over their fears, doubts, and challenges.

2. Journal what you have learnt about how to face your fear and doubt. This is necessary so you can go over them and apply them at a later date.

3. Memorise the verses of Scripture that talk about fear and doubt. There is a superpower that a verse hidden within brings. It puts you on the right track when you are going off due to fear and doubt.

4. Share what you have learnt with others at a fun club, or whatever means possible. What it does is that it energises you and keeps you encouraged even as you encourage others.

Other Ways to Overcome Fear and Doubt

1. Listen to good Christian music to lift up your spirit and encourage you.

2. Watch inspirational Christian videos to lift up your spirit and encourage you.

3. Encourage yourself from within, using positive inspirational and Christian words.

4. Get yourself busy with good pastimes and games. That way, your mind would be preoccupied and there would be no room for thoughts of fear and doubt.

5. Speak to trusted friends, family members, mentors and adults around you, and not naysayers. They will encourage you through your fears and doubts.

But We Can Fear Someone

"Fear of the LORD is the foundation of wisdom…"
–Proverbs 9:10

Yes! Only God! Because He is the Creator and Master of the Universe. And when we fear Him, we are showing Him reverence and He will give us a blessing–Wisdom.

The ways by which we fear God are:
* Reading and studying His Word
* Following His commands
* Pleasing Him with our lives and what we do

But we should never doubt God Almighty! And why is that?

God is not a man, so He does not lie. He is not human, so he does not change His mind. Has he ever spoken and failed to act? Has he ever promised and not carried it through?

–Numbers 23:19

He is not like us who say one thing today and say something else tomorrow. He is the same yesterday, today and forever. The Alpha and the Omega. The One who was and is and is to come. Therefore, you can trust and never doubt the One who has the whole world in the palm of His Hands.

Quick Reminder

FEAR	DOUBT
Fearful mindset	Do not give the
Endangers your	Opportunity to others to
Ability to	Underestimate you by
Rise strong	Believing naysayers that affect your
	Trust in God

Fill It Out

Write down and memorise seven verses each on fear and doubt, for each day of the week.

Write out a trusted person, adult or family member who would be your faith buddy, share your fears with them and seek counsel.

Try to stick with it for a month and see if there are changes in how you approach fear and doubt.

Day of the Week	Verse	Faith Buddy
e.g., Monday	**Fear:** *For God has not given us the spirit of fear and timidity, but of power, love, and self–discipline* **(2 Timothy 1:7)** **Doubt:** *But when you ask Him, be sure that your faith is in God alone. Do not waver, for a person with divided loyalty is as unsettled as a wave of sea that is blown and tossed by the wind* **(James 1:6)**	Mummy
Monday		
Tuesday		
Wednesday		
Thursday		

Friday		
Saturday		
Sunday		

EIGHT

Pride And Anger

There are six things the LORD hates—no seven things He detests: haughty eyes, a lying tongue, hands that kill the innocent, a heart that plots evil, feet that race to do wrong, a false witness who pours out lies, a person who sows discord in a family.

—Proverbs 6:16–19

From the list of things the LORD hates or detests, we see what comes first. Haughty eyes!

To have haughty eyes simply means to look down on others, because one thinks he is better than the other person. What bell does this ring? Pride you guess?

Well, there is a lesson here. Pride is one of the things the

LORD hates. Hence, we must run away from it at all costs. Much like fear comes with doubt, pride has a brother, which you guessed right! Anger! And he must also be avoided at all costs.

Let us deal with each of the themes separately before we link them all up. Shall we?

Pride

> *Pride: To be proud or feel bigger than usual when compared to people, things, or circumstances.*

Usually, when a person has pride, the person cannot be said to be humble. Pride and humility walk in opposite directions. Why? Because when one has humility, the person is simply very meek at heart and does not exalt himself, especially to make himself feel good or better than others.

What Pride Does

One thing pride does is to 'lift' a gentleman up in her head. Indeed, before a person starts to show actions of pride, it must have started in the person's mind with all sorts of ideas like:
- I am better than this other boy.
- Who does he think he is?
- I have been at the top of this class all my life. No one can come and take my place.

- I just cannot give in to this new leader of the swimming club. I do not think he has earned his place.
- And a whole lot of ideas that clearly do not come from God.

How Should You View Pride?

When dealing with pride, it is good to think about it this way.

God created us in His likeness, and did He create us to look down on the other human creations of His Hand? Absolutely not! So why then do we do that, knowingly or unknowingly? When we do that, in essence, we are just telling God that He is not a good creator and that He did not carefully evaluate to see His creation was good, before placing them on earth to live amongst us. And that is a very mean idea to have towards man and eventually towards God.

Anger

Anger: A feeling of displeasure towards something or someone.

He Got Angry

He was angry at his friend, because he disrespected him in front of the boys at the basketball club. He told himself, "I wouldn't let this go without a fight." And that was it! They started to trade words against each other. The rest was history. None of their peers were able to control them, and they had to report them to the school's disciplinary committee. They had bad reports written about them and the whole school got to find out. It was such an embarrassing situation.

If only he did not retaliate when his friend disgraced him in front of everyone. But really, that is what we are to do! It can be hard sometimes, especially when you are disgraced for no reason. But we have to understand that when we do not let our anger take control of us, we are having control over the negative things that it comes along with.

How Does Anger Manifest?

- **In negative emotions**, like using swear words, insulting, wishing people bad, having negative thoughts, and everything that comes with it.
- It causes **trouble** eventually.
- It leads to lots of **fighting and quarrelling.**
- And before you know it, many **people are hurt** due to the various expressions of anger.

Ben's Story

It was just a regular child game they were playing. No one was around, it was just Ben and his friend. Then they had a disagreement about the game. Ben let his anger get over him that he picked a camper's knife close by and attempted pushing it through the abdomen of his friend. What saved him? His friend had a buckle on, at that side of his body. When the knife did not go through his friend's body, he realised that he had almost made a mess of himself and would have been on his way to reform school, but for the buckle.

Did You Know That Anger Can Be transferred?

From the story of the two boys, we see that anger can be transferred if we do not realise it early enough. In his defence, he started to show a bad attitude, so he does not look weak before the others. He thought that his solution was retaliating in anger. Not knowing, his friend had just transferred that same anger to him. And of course, the anger came with pride because none of them were ready to take a step back and let things go. They both wanted to prove a point that they were better than each other and deserved to be treated better (which was true), but they wanted to bring each other down, and that was the point pride manifested!

Pride And Anger Are Siblings

Pride definitely moves with anger, and they both lead to destruction. Some people refer to pride in an extreme way–*arrogance*.

When you are so proud, that you throw your weight around and are ready to impose yourself on others, or if you have to show bad attitudes of being dominating in speech or action, then you are exhibiting extreme pride, which is arrogance, and could potentially lead to anger depending on the situation.

They go together, just perfectly, and overcoming one is the step to overcoming the other.

What Does GOD Say About PRIDE and ANGER?

PRIDE	
Isaiah 2:12	*For the LORD of Heaven's Armies has a day of reckoning. He will punish the **proud** and mighty and bring down everything that is exalted.* **God Says:** There is a punishment for all those who are proud and puffed up. God hates anything that tries to exalt itself above Him and all the things He has created.

James 4:6	*And He gives grace generously. As the Scriptures say, "God opposes the **proud** but gives grace to the **humble**."* **God Says:** He only listens and answers the prayers of those who are humble. Humble yourself in His presence and before people and receive your breakthrough.
James 4:10	***Humble** yourself before the LORD, and He will lift you up in honour.* **God Says:** He only lifts and places in positions of honour those who are humble.
Jeremiah 9:23	*This is what the LORD says: "Don't let the wise **boast** in their wisdom, or the powerful **boast** in their power, or the rich **boast** in their riches."* **God Says:** If you boost in the wisdom, power, and riches that He has blessed you with, as if they were yours, you are being unwise and proud. Do not boast about the blessings of God as though you got them for yourself.

Philippians 2:3	*Do not be selfish; do not try to impress others.* ***Be humble***, *thinking of others better than yourselves.* **God Says:** One way to be humble is to think that there is always someone who may be better than you in a particular area. That way, you will be ready to learn new things.
ANGER	
Psalm 37:8	*Stop being **angry**! Turn from your rage! Do not lose your temper—it only leads to harm.* **God Says:** Nothing good ever comes from expressed anger. It just leads to difficult situations.
Psalm 86:15	*But you, O LORD, are a God of compassion and mercy, slow to get **angry** and failed with unfailing love and faithfulness.* **God Says:** If we say we are like Him, then we should be slow to anger like He is and have more of love and respect for others.

Proverbs 15:1	*A gentle answer deflects **anger**, but harsh words make tempers flare.* **God Says:** One way that anger gets out of control is when we speak to people in a harsh manner. Talk to people in a calm manner. They might even listen to you better.
Proverbs 22:24	*Do not befriend **angry** people or associate with hot–tempered people, or you will learn to be like them and endanger your soul.* **God Says:** You become who you follow. If you befriend people who are always angry, in no time, you will be tagged the same way.
Ephesians 4:26–27	*And "do not sin by letting **anger** control you." Do not let the sun go down while you are still **angry**, for **anger** gives a foothold to the devil.* **God Says:** When we let anger control us, we are sinning, and we would give the devil control over our lives to do as He pleases.

How To Get Rid Of This Pair

1. **Pride:** Do not think too highly of yourself, that you look down on others and think that you are better than

them. This is pride and leads to arrogance, which leads to expressing anger.

2. **Anger:** Do not be quick to talk, especially when you are not treated right, or you are being talked to wrongly. This is what you can do:

- Hold yourself calmly.
- Think before you speak, because when you are angered, the initial words that come from your mouth may not be constructed well.
- Walk away from the scene so that you are not provoked.
- Only speak to a trusted adult on how you felt, not people who will encourage you to do bad.

3. Ask God for the grace to stand firm against pride and anger because they lead to destruction and so many downfalls. You can do this through prayer.

ANGER	PRIDE
Actively	Purposely
Notice causes of anger to	Resist
Guide and	It (Pride) as it is a
Encourage you to	Danger to your
Resist it (Anger)	Existence

Fill It Out

Follow the example in the table below and state an experience each day where you gave in to anger and pride.

Try this out for one month and evaluate yourself, by checking if you are improving over your anger and pride. It is possible!

Day of the Week	Situation	Did I retaliate?	Prayer for the Next Day
e.g., Monday	I was bullied at school by the senior boys	Yes, I exhibited anger by lashing out	Dear LORD, help me not to lash out when angered at school
Monday			
Tuesday			

Wednesday			
Thursday			
Friday			
Saturday			
Sunday			

NINE

Envy And Jealousy

Envy: To feel unhappy because someone is enjoying some benefits that you are not experiencing. Sometimes, it is called covetousness, meaning that you wish to have what the other person has.

Jealousy: Being hostile towards a person because they are believed to be at an advantage, because of who they are or what they have.

The Distinction

Some people may be envious of a person, but still act cool with the person. Jealousy is more severe because a person may act in a hostile manner to another person and make it clear to that person that they are not happy with them.

God Should Also Be Pleased With My Sacrifice!

> "Why did God reject my sacrifice and accept my brother's? I gave God His offering in the way He requires it but He still picked Abel's offering over mine. Could it be that God prefers Abel to me? But I am older! I should be preferred over my brother. Maybe I should take his life so that God will be left with no option but to like me and accept all my sacrifices going forward", said Cain.

> [A few moments later]

> "Cain! Where is your brother?", said God.

> "Am I supposed to be my brother's keeper?"

> "Because you killed your own brother, I will punish you for all the world to see"

The story above was taken from the Bible, *Genesis 4:1–18*? This is a classic example of how far envy and jealousy can go. Cain thought that God preferred Abel to him out of envy, forgetting that God created them both and should love them in the same way. He thought killing his brother would save the situation, but it ended in a curse on him.

What we need to realise is that envy and jealousy go together.

They complement each other. There is not one without the other. And for every act of envy and jealousy, there are certainly causes.

The Root Of Envy And Jealousy

- Lack of contentment: Not being satisfied with the many things God has blessed us with. This makes us look over our shoulders and think that others are doing better, especially when we think they are more blessed and what they have looks better than what God has given us.

- Lack of understanding of God's plan for one's life and the purpose for which we are on earth: It makes us look on other people's lives and purposes as if they are best, we envy and wish that we were the ones living it out. Meanwhile, God may have a master plan for them but because they are too busy to discover it, they keep envying others.

Read Chapter 4 (Potential to Purpose) to understand better how to discover God's plan for your life.

The Fruit Of Envy And Jealousy

- Resentment and unnecessary anger towards people.

- Lack of Joy–because you will be concentrating on others and be thinking that your situation is bad, that you lose your happiness and think that all is not well with you.

- Picking up bad habits–like covetousness, complaining, being a naysayer, wishing people bad, gossiping, backbiting and spreading false information about people, and a whole lot.

- Inability to hear from God clearly–because your mind may be filled with all sorts of negative thoughts.

- Missing out on God's plan and purpose for one's life–Much like fear and doubt as well as pride and anger, this pair (envy and jealousy) does not come with anything proper to give a person. This is the reason we should flee from it.

What Does GOD Say About ENVY And JEALOUSY?

ENVY	
Proverbs 14:30	*A peaceful heart leads to a healthy body;* ***envy*** *is like cancer in the bones.* **God Says:** Envy destroys our health. It makes us overthink which could lead to mental health issues. Do not encourage it.

Mark 7:21–23	*For from within, out of a person's heart, come evil thoughts,…, **envy**, slander, pride, and foolishness. All these vile things come from within; they are what defile you."* **God Says:** Envy is an evil thought. If you want to live your life pleasing God, you do not have to encourage it.
Proverbs 23:17–18	*Do not **envy** sinners, but always continue to fear the LORD. You will be rewarded for this; your hope will not be disappointed.* *God Says:* Do not envy people who do wrong things, especially when it seems they are advancing in what they are doing. Place your hope and faith in God and He will give you your clean portion of blessings.
Exodus 20:17	*Do not **covet** your neighbour's house (and property).* **God Says:** Just do not envy what your neighbour or someone close by has, for which you do not have. Why? Because He has a perfect plan for every person.

1 Corinthians 13:4	*Love is patient and kind. Love is not envious…* **God Says:** We cannot say we have love in us when we are envious of people and what they possess. If you find yourself envious of another, it shows that you do not have that much love towards the person. If you are in that situation, ask God for the Grace to love the person regardless.
JEALOUSY	
Job 5:2	*Surely resentment destroys the fool, and **jealousy** kills the simple.* **God Says:** The presence of jealousy shows that we are not wise, and lack of wisdom can destroy a person.
Proverbs 27:4	*Anger is cruel, and wrath is like a flood, but **jealousy** is even more dangerous.* **God Says:** Jealousy is even more dangerous than anger. It should be avoided.

James 3:14–16	*But if you are bitterly jealous and there is selfish ambition in your heart, do not cover up the truth with boosting and lying. For **jealousy** and selfishness are not God's kind of wisdom. Such things are earthly, unspiritual, and demonic. For wherever there is **jealousy** and selfish ambition, there you will find disorder and evil of every kind.* **God Says:** Jealousy comes with selfishness and God does not like these because they come with all sorts of negative emotions, like disorderliness and evil. We should avoid jealousy at all costs.
Galatians 5:19–21	*When you follow the desires of your sinful nature, the results are very clear: sexual immorality, impurity,…, quarrelling, **jealousy**, outbursts of anger, selfish ambition,…, envy,…and other sins like these. Let me tell you again, as I have before, that anyone living that sort of life will not inherit the Kingdom of God.* **God Says:** Jealousy is a sin, and it will prevent us from communing with God eternally. Hence, it must be avoided totally.

1 Corinthians 3:3	*For you are still controlled by your sinful nature. You are **jealous** of one another and quarrel with each other. Doesn't that prove you are controlled by your sinful nature? Aren't you living like the people of the world?* **God Says:** Exhibiting jealousy is proof that we are no different from those in the world who are not saved. Distinguish yourself from those in the world by avoiding jealousy of any form.

How To Practically Flee From Envy and Jealousy

1. Practice the act of having good thoughts towards all people–Anytime a negative thought comes to mind, choose to focus on the good things the person has done. Always remember that you are not Jesus Christ, and you have no authority to judge a person, irrespective of the circumstance.

2. Read God's Word to know His promises towards you–This way, you would have no room to be envious and jealous of another person because:

•   You will understand that each person's life is different and crafted by God.

- You will be so busy pursuing your dreams, goals and purpose that you would not find the time to throw a pity–party to express how you feel left behind and envious or jealous of another person.

3. Remember the Golden Rule – Before you are envious or jealous of someone, ask yourself if you would have been happy to be receiving such a bad emotion. If your answer is 'no', then you will be guided on what to do to others.

4. Practice the act of gratitude and thankfulness–God never makes mistakes. All He does is perfect and holy. Hence, every person created is a masterpiece of God. When you think this way, joy automatically floods your heart because you know that God has got your back and you will be thankful to Him. You will have no room for a pity–party with friends, that will lead to envy and jealousy.

Way To Go

The truth of the matter is that as we grow, some of our friends will reach their life's purposes and destinations faster than others. It only means that we are different and unique people on this journey of life. Do not let the negative thoughts of Satan fill your mind. Rather, focus on discovering your purpose, if you have not done so, and live in it. That way, being envious and jealous of someone will be a tedious chore for you.

ENVY	JEALOUSY
Entertaining	Just
Negative and	Exhibit a positive
Vile thoughts towards people rob	Attitude of
	Loving people
You of your joy	Openly and genuinely to encourage
	Unity and to
	Spread joy so
	You are always happy

Fill It Out

Write down and memorise seven verses each on envy and jealousy, for each day of the week.

Write out a trusted person, adult or family member who would be your love buddy, share your envious and jealous moments with them and seek counsel on how to be a better person.

Try to stick with it for a month and see if there are changes in how you approach envious and jealous situations.

Day of the Week	Verse	Love Buddy
e.g., Monday	**Envy:** *Do not **covet** your neighbour's house (and property) (**Exodus 20:17**)* **Jealousy:** *Anger is cruel, and wrath is like a flood, but jealousy is even more dangerous (**Proverbs 27:4**)*	Daddy

Monday		
Tuesday		
Wednesday		
Thursday		
Friday		
Saturday		
Sunday		

PART 4

The Josephs In The Bible

THE BIBLE IS THE MOST inspirational, motivational, informative and transformational book one could ever read. It's the ultimate source of God's Word. You could read or hear God's Word from other sources but none can compare with the Bible. Oh! The Bible is full of treasures.

There's virtually nothing happening in the world or happening to you today that is new. Everyone faces challenges in life regardless of their age. This also tells us that every boy who would become the pride of nations can accept not only the good times but the challenging times as well. Learning how to embrace the good times while walking through challenging times and emerging stronger is what makes you an exceptional leader.

You might have heard a couple of times, people ask or probably you have also thought about it, "If God is really God, why does He allow bad things to happen to good people?"

The Bible has records of gentlemen and ladies who became exceptional leaders despite their challenging situations. We will look at some of these people and from them we will be able to conclude on whether we have to go through tough situations to emerge as great leaders or not.

In this section we will be talking about:
10.   Paul–The Authentic Leader
11.   Daughters of Zelophehad–The United Ladies
12.   Joseph–The Compassionate Leader

CHAPTER TEN

Paul

The AUTHENTIC Leader

People love to relate with someone who is authentic, in other words, someone who is genuine.

An authentic person is a person who is not afraid to be true to who they are, including their personality, values, and principles in life. They simply stick to who they are regardless of what others think of them.

Looking at the story of Paul formerly known as Saul, he was a man found to be passionate and diligent in the things that displeased God. Just as God has a special purpose for you and I, He transformed Saul into a new man, Paul and set him on

His own agenda.

Here Comes The Bully

> He is so full of himself that he looks down on anyone who is not in his rank. He is a racist, who not only despises those that do not belong to his racial group, religion or rank but also imprisons them because of his authority. He is not concerned whether people are hurting in any way, all he wants out of life is to see that anyone he hates doesn't see any good about their lives.

Above is the story of Saul described in a nutshell. His life was completely in the mess of bullying. If you have been bullied, you would understand what it really feels like.

> *In simple terms, bullying means intentional and consistent acts of hurting others or being mean to others.*

> *A bully is a person who intentionally and consistently hurts or harms someone.*

Bullying could be expressed in different ways, but we will be looking at four, which are common among tweens and teens.

1. **Verbal Bullying:** This is the act of insulting someone with negative, offensive or abusive words. It involves inappropriate use of words. A lot of people bully verbally but they fail to admit they are bullying. A lot of young boys also suffer depression or try to hurt themselves as a result of unpleasant words or names they are being called.

2. **Physical Bullying:** This is the act of hitting, kicking, punching, slapping, pushing or pulling someone. You also need to pay attention to any thing or situation that causes you to act out your anger. Anger is not a sin, but it becomes a sin when you allow it to control or manage you.

3. **Cyber Bullying:** This is a form of bullying or harassment using electronic means. It involves the use of digital and social media platforms to threaten or disgrace someone by sending embarrassing messages or information. Cyber bullying is as destructive or even more destructive than other forms of bullying. Any information sent on some of the social media platforms are seen by millions of people. You may think, after all, the person is not with you, but it's more than what you think. Victims of cyberbullying may succumb to depression, anxiety and other stress–related conditions.

4. **Sexual Bullying:** This is the act of exposing someone to things that affect their sexuality negatively. This

may also include touching someone's private parts or body shaming.

Saul was heavily involved in bullying verbally and physically. He strongly believed no one could call him to order. However, in the midst of the deep mess, an opportunity for a new life was introduced to him. As a boy growing to become a future leader, what are your struggles or weaknesses? Or probably you are the one being bullied, and you have lost your self–esteem, there's good news for you.

Can God Really Use Me?

It is not what you think! The people God uses are not those who are already made. It is not based on age, height, colour, stature, grade, intellect or culture. God chooses and uses everyone regardless of who they are. See what the Bible says:

> *Instead, God chose things the world considers foolish in order to shame those who think they are wise. And He chose things that are powerless to shame those who are powerful.*
> *–1 Corinthians 1:27*

However, to be on God's agenda, you need two qualifications:

1.   **Acceptance:** You need to be true to yourself by identifying your strengths and weaknesses. Saul knew his

strengths were courage and great influence while his weakness was bullying (persecution). He decided to let go of his weakness and chose to release his strength to God for His use.

No matter who you are, you have your area of strength and that is what God is looking for. However, God will not force you to release your strength if you are not willing to and He will not force you to accept His offer. You also need to know that when God places you on His agenda, He does not only act on your strength, He also exchanges your strength for His supernatural strength called GRACE.

2.   **Brokenness:** This comes after you have identified and admitted your strengths and weaknesses.

This does not mean you are a sinner. You might have a weakness like any of the ones already mentioned in Part Three–fear, doubt, pride, anger, envy, jealousy. It could be prayerlessness, low self esteem or probably you are addicted to TV, games or other things. Anything that is affecting your relationship with God and people is a weakness. It could

Brokenness is a state of allowing God to work on your weaknesses and transform you from who you are into who He wants you to be.

also be that you need more of God and you want Him to search your heart so He can blot out anything that would not allow His glory to find expression in your life. As a boy becoming a well–rounded leader, you must make this a daily practice–asking God to search your heart. This Scripture could be added to your daily prayer:

> *"Search me, O God, and know my heart; test me and know my anxious thoughts. Point out anything in me that offends you, and lead me along the path of everlasting life."*
>
> *–Psalm 139:23–24*

Do Not Look Down on Yourself

The authentic leader–Paul did not look down on himself, despite his horrible past. He didn't have a mindset that everyone who comes his way would judge or accuse him. If he had thought that way, probably, he wouldn't have accepted the offer of a fresh start Jesus introduced to him and he would have missed a lifetime of salvation and exploits for God.

Always bear in mind that even if God puts anyone on His agenda, it takes the broken to complete the tasks He gives and it takes the broken to finish well.

Your ability or skill is not meant to be looked down on either. Be true to yourself and accept who you are. If you separate yourself from who you are currently, you can't be called an authentic leader and the moment you start thinking less of yourself the moment you allow people to do the same to you.

Five Things Happen When You Look Down on Yourself
1. You see only your weaknesses.
2. You will not be able to see good in any opportunity.
3. You think no one has something good to offer.
4. You remain where you are.
5. You will not be able to live out your purpose.

Saul jumped at the lifetime opportunity and was ready to go all the way becoming the person God called him to be.

Your Defining Moment

> *Immediately, something like scales fell from Saul's eyes, and he could see again. He got up and was baptized, and after taking some food, he regained his strength. Saul spent several days with the disciples in Damascus.*
>
> *—Acts 9:18–20*

The moment the scales fell off his eyes, Saul knew that was his defining moment, he knew the scales represent his years of bullying, he knew it was the start of a new life and he must have sensed that might be his last chance of identifying with the Lord Jesus Christ, His

An authentic leader is one who lives a life of integrity, someone who does not hide his true picture and is willing to do all it takes to become the well rounded version of himself.

power and His people. He made a decision, he got up and was baptised to be on the Lord's side. What a decision!

> 'The Oak Inside the Acorn' written by Max Lucado, is a story about a little Acorn who would have loved to stay with her mother forever. An opportunity came when she found herself in the midst of a completely different environment, culture and peers. Her defining moment came when she realised she wasn't made to look like anyone but to accept who she was, ask for necessary help to grow and fulfill her purpose even in the midst of a foreign culture.

Maybe you are wondering, what else would the purpose of a seed be? The purpose of the little Acorn that later became a big Oak tree was to provide shade for children when they are on the playground and to keep the heat of the sun from tanning or burning their skin. In a nutshell, her one purpose was to 'save'.

Now, what is your defining moment?

1. The day the scales of sins fall off your eyes and you accept Jesus Christ to become your Saviour and Lord. If you are still reading this book and you have not accepted Him, the time to take the decision is now. Pause now and go to Chapter Two, say the salvation

prayer with all your heart and start walking in the Light.

2. The day you discover the purpose of God for your life and you are ready to embark on the journey to fulfil it.

3. The Day you realise how powerful God is and you make up your mind to stay on His side even if people misunderstand you.

4. The day you surrender your identity to God by asking Him to hold your hands and lead you wherever He plans to take you.

5. The day you make a decision to rise and fly above all limitations, challenges and weaknesses.

6. The day you hold someone's hand and guide him step by step through fulfilling the purpose of God for his life.

7. The day your one goal in life is not only to save yourself but to save others.

What Would You Be Remembered For?

As you grow into a well–rounded leader, the decision you make today counts, whether good or wrong. And the result of that decision will not only affect you and your loved ones but also the nations.

The story of Paul renamed from Saul is one that sounds unbelievable but true. Who could have thought someone who had no regard for God, His power and His people would be greatly used by God. In your journey through life, you may encounter people who would look at you and paint a false picture about you based on the wrong things you have done.

Today, we remember Paul, whenever we talk about great leaders and apostles. Because of the lifetime opportunity he seized and the decision he made, Paul was able to turn the hearts of many to God, he raised many godly leaders, he performed many and mighty miracles and fulfilled the purpose of God for his life excellently. Let's look at what the Bible says about the miracles of Paul:

However, know this, the person you become can only be determined by God and the choices you make.

> *God gave Paul the power to perform unusual miracles. so that even handkerchiefs and aprons that had touched him were taken to the sick, and their illnesses were cured and the evil spirits left them.*
>
> *—Acts 19:12–13*

Leadership Nuggets From Paul

A–Accurate. He was always sensitive to God's voice and that guided the choices he made.

U–Understanding. He paid attention to understand the

condition of the people he led.

T–Thankful. He always gave gratitude to God for his new life and also to people for their generous giving to him.

H–Hardworking. He never stayed idle or did something worthless. He always went after his goal with a winning mindset.

E–Encourager. He was a man of the people, loving, caring and sharing the burdens of the people he led.

N–No–quitting. He was a goal getter, he never gave up until he reached his goal.

T–Teacher. He taught the truth of God's Word, he mentored and raised leaders, and he did this so well because he was a prayerful man.

I–Integrity. He was a man of his word, he kept to his word and lived by what he said.

C–Courage. He spoke about Christ everywhere he found himself, without fear of being arrested.

Fill It Out

How do you see opportunities? Something to cherish or despise?

_____

_____

What decision are you making today?

_____

_____

Will this decision have a positive or negative impact on you or anyone?

_____

_____

Write down your legacy, "What do you want to be known for?"

_____

_____

_____

_____

Write this scripture out on a postcard, paste it somewhere you can easily see and say it every day - "Don't let anyone look down on you (insert your name) because you are young but set an example for the believers in speech, in conduct, in love, in faith and purity." - Timothy 4:12

_____

_____

_____

_____

_____

_____

CHAPTER ELEVEN

Daughters Of Zelophehad

Mahlah Noah Hoglah Milcah Tirzah
The UNITED Ladies

Zelophehad's daughters belonged to the family groups of Manasseh, son of Joseph. The daughters' names were Mahlah, Noah, Hoglah, Milcah and Tirzah. They went to the entrance of the Meeting Tent. There they stood before Moses, Eleazar the priest, the leaders and all the people. They said, "Our father died in the desert. He was not one of Korah's followers who came against the Lord. Our father died because of his own sin. But he had no sons. Our father's name will die out because he had no sons. Give us property among our father's relatives."

So, Moses brought their case to the Lord. The Lord

said to him, "The daughters of Zelophehad are right. They should get what their father owned. Give them property among their father's relatives. "Tell the Israelites, 'If a man dies and has no son, then everything he owns should go to his daughter. If he has no daughter, then everything he owns should go to his brothers. If he has no brothers, then everything he owns should go to his father's brothers. If his father has no brothers, then everything he owns should go to the nearest relative in his family group. This should be a rule among the people of Israel as the Lord has given this command to Moses."

–Numbers 27:1–11

One Voice

The story of the five sisters you just read should leave every reader, especially someone who has a sibling in awe. For the five of them to work in agreement, without one seeking to be the one who would take the lion share if God gave them victory, is a mystery. This is not an act that is common among many siblings. They were all ready to speak with one voice. Speaking up to claim their entitlement must have been the idea of one person but they all agreed.

Moses made a request to God on behalf of the five sisters and God honoured the request. God must have honoured their request based on something He saw among them, 'UNITY'. The Bible tells us in Amos 3:3 that, *"Two people cannot work together except they have agreed to do so."* What can we then say about five people?

To become a purposeful leader, unity must be one of your core values. You must be ready to let go of pride at all costs. People can listen to you out of fear or simple obedience, but they would not stay long with you before they turn their back on you if you are full of pride. As in the case of the daughters of Zelophehad, it didn't really matter to them who came up with the idea, all they saw was a good idea and they were all ready to fight for their right. Note here also, that the person who brought up the idea was not asked to go after it all alone, they all agreed. They had one voice.

How did they even present their case before Moses and other leaders? Did they speak one by one or was it rendered in chorus?

Did they present their case like two young siblings, ages 4 and 7? Whenever they are on the phone speaking to their grannies, they say almost everything in chorus. Little caution to ask them to speak one after another, is like adding fuel to the fire. They never plan it but you wonder how they do it.

Speak Up

"Don't let anyone look down on you because you are young, but set an example for the believers in speech, in conduct, in love, in faith and in purity."
—1 Timothy 4:12

Do you belong to a group, team, family? Do you have an idea to do something? Do you keep the idea to yourself? Are you planning to go after the idea without sharing it with anyone? What do you stand to gain or lose if you share the idea with the people that matter to you?

Above are the questions you must ask yourself whenever an idea pops up in your mind. Your idea could be but not limited to learning a skill, starting something new or sharing information. Ideas will always flow through your mind. Many times, people have good ideas that will benefit them and the entire group, but they decide not to share. They would rather watch someone else come up with the same idea than putting theirs forward.

Reasons People Do Not Share Their Ideas

There are several reasons people keep their ideas to themselves and we are going to look at five of them.

- **Fear:** Fear makes people think their idea is worthless, hence it silences their voice. To accomplish anything good for yourself and become the leader God wants you to be, fear is one of the limiting obstacles to deal with. It doesn't mean you wouldn't be afraid after dealing with every fear that comes, it only means you can always do whatever you set your mind to do even in the face of fear, and this attitude is known as a winning attitude.

- **Doubt:** This is filled with 'What if's...' What if my idea doesn't make sense? What if no one believes me? What if no one listens to me? What if they think less of me because I am young? What if no one is ready to support me? What if I am the only one thinking that way? The 'What if's' list is endless.

- **Selfishness:** Someone might decide not to share his ideas because he has seen that it is going to bring him lots of benefits or fame, to be known as the first person who stepped out to do it. The eldest–Mahla *(just a guess as their names are arranged in the Bible)* or the one who brought up the idea to speak to Moses and the leaders about their right, could have taught to go behind the rest to claim their father's inheritance. She could have thought if she won, she would only give her sisters a small portion while she takes the lion share. But she chose to share the idea with others without a selfish mindset.

- **Not ready to take on responsibility:** Sharing your

ideas with your team or a group might come with commitment. In some cases, people only need your idea to run with and you don't have to be responsible for how it will be actualised. However, if you present an idea in a team, you might be asked to take it up, while others support you. Sometimes, the 'idea presenter' is not ready to commit to this role because of the hard work it requires.

- **Someone might make it their idea:** Couple of times, we've heard people say, I don't want to share my idea with anyone because I don't want people to take ownership of it. They decide not to share their ideas even with trusted people and if care is not taken, they might end up not making the most of that idea. There have been cases whereby people didn't share their ideas with anyone, till it was late and the ideas remained as they were, with no fruits to show for it.

Do you have a big dream or idea? A boy who has a big dream or idea must be ready to deal with fear and doubt. You must not allow selfishness to hold you back from sharing your ideas, because if you do all you're meant to do, gain is the result. Oh! You must be ready to take on responsibility and be committed to it. Also, it shouldn't bother you who wants to steal or own your idea, God is the one who gives ideas, He never runs out of them and He is always looking for people He can trust them with. So, look up to Him and He will give you the idea that has your name stamped on.

Four S' to Look out for
When Sharing Your Idea

The steps that will be discussed below are some of the steps taken at Elegant Initiatives, to turn the idea God gave us–'Starting a mentoring group, to grow well–rounded leaders globally'into a masterpiece. The idea was given to one person, she prayed about it, she perceived it was God's gift, which made it **sensible**. She **shared** it with trusted people from a **sincere** heart and she started following through, giving her full **support.**

1.   **Sensible:** As mentioned earlier, loads of ideas flow through our minds but there's a saying that, "Not all that glitters is gold." The same goes for those ideas that you've got. Some of them make you feel good already, others ring in your ears often as if success is just the next thing you see at a blink. After praying about your idea, search the Word of God to see what God says about that idea and hold on to whatever He says.

Though the daughters of Zelophehad had a reasonable idea, if God had not backed them up, their idea would have been like every other idea, and it would have been fruitless.

2.   **Share:** Never jump into sharing your idea because you think it's reasonable or because you want to be awarded the famous idea–giver. Leaders don't act like that. You need to be sensitive to your environment, team or the group you

belong to, and you need to know the right time to share your idea. This does not mean you should wait for a perfect time, because a perfect time may never arrive, but when the right time comes you will know.

3.　　**Sincere:** Looking at the daughters of Zelophehad, we would see that whoever the idea must have come from had a sincere heart. She shared the idea with her sisters from a sincere heart. That made the idea authentic and others accepted it. Please bear in mind that people may not accept your idea for several reasons, and this is where you need to take the lead. Believe in yourself, never look down on the idea because God has not only stamped your name on it, but He has also added His signature.

4.　　**Support:** Supporting one another to transform the idea into a masterpiece is very key. As the pride of nations that you are becoming, you must be ready to follow through with the idea you shared. We also see this in the daughters of Zelophehad, they followed through to breakthrough. The transformation of your idea into a masterpiece wouldn't happen overnight, you need to build a day at a time. You also need to understand that your way may not be the best way at all times, look out for the possible best ideas or ways offered by others, while you work together in patience and unity.

The New Normal

The daughters of Zelophehad presented their case to Moses, who went ahead to pray and ask God for what to do. God granted their heart desire and through them a new rule in favoured of every female orphan was made by God. The rule became the new normal.

Sometimes, the person God wants you to speak to for advice may or may not be a believer, but when you have a good relationship with God, you would know who to speak to whenever you need to. It could be a professional counsellor or someone He knows will not hurt or take advantage of you. Working in unity with the other people He connects you with is one of the sure ways He makes you victorious.

If you have siblings, especially girls, see them as a gift from God. There are so many unpleasant ways life treats females, and you might be their only saviour in hard times. Speak up for them when necessary, never look down on them or their opinion and see to it that you are not divided, so you can all do exploits together.

Leadership Nuggets From The Daughters Of Zelophehad

U–Understanding is important in any relationship to build a masterpiece.

N–No difficult challenge can sweep over you if you don't give up.

I–Ideas not expressed following the four S' may never be fruitful.

T–Trust God and let Him be the foundation on whom you trust people.

E–Express your mind by speaking up to trusted people like Moses.

D–Deal with fear, doubt and selfishness because they are killers of dreams.

Fill it Out

In one word, describe the daughters of Zelophehad.

_____

_____

_____

_____

Do you have an idea or dream? Write it down.

_____

_____

_____

_____

Mention THREE things that are holding you back from sharing your idea, then speak to a trusted person about them.

_____

_____

_____

_____

_____

State THREE things you can start doing to work in unity with others.

_____

_____

_____

_____

Write this Scripture out on a postcard, paste it somewhere you can easily see and say it every day: *"I appeal to you, brothers and sisters, in the name of our Lord Jesus Christ, that all of you agree with one another in what you say and that there be no divisions among you, but that you be perfectly united in mind and thought."–1 Corinthians 1:10*

TWELVE

Joseph

The COMPASSIONATE Leader
7 Days Devotional Guide

Having journeyed through eleven chapters, we would like you to slow down, take a day at a time as you learn about COMPASSION. We know you now have the passion to become the pride of nations, but it takes passion and compassion to become one.

If you don't have compassion for the people you meet on your way to becoming a leader, you will only struggle with no positive result to show for your effort. There are times in life that you will be hurting and you will encounter someone who is also hurting. Other times you may need help and see someone who also needs help. It takes compassion to be able to put them ahead of you to offer help, amid your pains or difficulties.

Another word for Compassion is 'Love'. To become a purposeful leader, you need to show love. The Bible tells us in *1 Corinthians 13:1* that:

> *"If I speak with the tongues of men and of angels, but have not love [for others growing out of God's love for me], then I have become only a noisy gong or a clanging cymbal [just an annoying distraction]."*

You are encouraged to take your time in the next seven days, as you go through this devotional and we believe you will be greatly empowered.

DAY 1

Read Genesis 37:1–11

THE FAVORITE

Joseph was Jacob's favorite out of twelve sons. This was so obvious to the extent that the father made a special and beautiful robe for him. When his brothers realised the excess love their father had for him, they were so jealous. One day, father sent Joseph to look after his brothers where they were pasturing the flock. Joseph was so excited to see his brothers, that he shared his dreams with them and that got them even more jealous.

Know This

Jacob trusted Joseph to always come back with a report on the exact proceedings on the field. Joseph built his reputation in the sight of his father as a very trustworthy person. How do people see you? Do they know you to tell the truth as it is? Can your parents count on you?

Sometimes, people will hate you in life when you are different or preferred. But you always have to remember to stay humble.

We have to be careful who we share our dreams with. Some people may not understand your dream, and that is fine. Do not let anyone's negative comment on your dreams deter you from moving forward. That is why you must be careful to share your dreams with only those who will be willing to encourage you and help you achieve them.

Declaration For Today

I will always stay humble and respect others regardless of me being different or preferred over them.

Verse For Today

Behold, I am sending you out as sheep in the midst of wolves, so be wise as serpents and innocent as doves.–Matthew 10:16

Fill It Out

Identify one thing that makes you special.	
How have you been treated because of this special trait in you?	
Write five things you can start doing that will help you to stand by your values, no matter what you go through in life.	
Write out one Bible verse that can guide you to stand by your values.	

DAY 2

Read Genesis 37:12–36

JOSEPH'S TRASH EXPERIENCE

"Ha! Father, where are you? Pa, pa... (stuttering), Pa Jacob, are you there? It's your son, Joe, yes your favorite! Dad, I know you are miles away from here, bu bu bu buuuuuuut... can you just whisper... Reuben ... elder ..., don't allow this to happen to me, plea ... plea ... plea ... ase" Hmmm! Guess these and more were the thoughts and words flowing through Joseph's mind and mouth respectively while in the pit. Joseph could have thought, "One day very soon I would find my way home to my father." Contrary to his thought, it was the beginning of many years of trash experiences for him.

There would be lots of circumstances we might not be able to control as long as we live on the earth. Many of us desire to become the Pride of nations but no one would ever for once desire to go through unpleasant situations to become one.

Remember, from yesterday's story, Joseph was so excited when he saw his brothers that he shared his dreams with them. They became so jealous and hated him more, then the unexpected happened. His brothers seized him, put him in a pit and sold Him into slavery. Joseph did not desire to go on the sudden and unpleasant journey his brothers forcefully sent him. Have you ever wondered, "How on earth would one's brothers do such a thing to their brother?"

Know This

Whatever you go through in life, you are not alone. God is always there with you, He knows and sees all you are going through because He is the All–knowing and All–seeing God **(Omniscient).**

Even if your friends or loved ones are not bold enough to rescue you from danger or speak up for you, speak to God, He's ever–ready to help because his power is unlimited **(Omnipotent).**

Joseph's father could not hear the voice of his favorite son because he was far away, but God heard him. God hears every whisper you make because He is ever–present **(Omnipresent).**

Declaration

I declare that no weapon formed against me shall prosper and no plan of man will ever limit me from becoming who I was created to be in Jesus' name.

Verse For Today

When you pass through the waters, I will be with you; and when you pass through the rivers, they will not sweep over you. When you walk through the fire, you will not be burned; the flames will not set you ablaze.–Isaiah 43:2

Fill It Out

If you were Joseph and it looks like God doesn't show up immediately to help you, what would you do?	
Write out the meaning of each of the following names that describe God: Omniscient Omnipotent Omnipresent	
Search the Scripture and write out a verse that tells you that God is your present help in times of need.	

DAY 3

Read Genesis 39:1-20

RUN FOR YOUR LIFE

WHAT WOULD YOU HAVE THOUGHT would happen to Joseph after being sold? *"Asked to do all kinds of hard labour? Deprived of food? Beaten and wounded?"* Your guess is as good as ours! To our amazement, Joseph was bought into wealth and not only that, every asset in Potiphar's house was kept in his care.

Someone reading this might be saying "Oh! I don't lie, bully, steal or engage in any ungodly act, I should be free from trouble." Whenever we make a decision to do only what is right, we expect to enjoy a life free of troubles. Hmmm! But it is not always so. Joseph was faced with another trash when Potiphar's wife wanted to commit sin with him. Joseph, knowing that that doesn't look like the dream he saw, made up his mind to do only what was right. He said NO to Potiphar's wife and ran for his life. Just like what any other person would do, when his master, Potiphar heard what happened, he believed his wife and commanded Joseph to be locked up in prison–additional trash!

Know This

If you desire to become the person God wants you to be, then you need to make up your mind not to settle for anything that's not in the plan of God for you.

If anyone (female, male, old, young...) asks you to do anything ungodly, be bold to say 'NO' and stay away from them if they persist.

It is better to be punished for what you didn't do than to enjoy a moment of sin, thereby truncating the plan of God for your life. That sounds hard, right? Always do what is right, because there's always a big eye watching you.

The problems we go through are meant to mold us and not mess us up. Sandy Smith says, *"God allows pain so that we might learn to trust His faithfulness, sufficiency and tender love to us."*

Declaration

No matter what I go through in life, I will not settle for anything that does not align with the purpose of God for me and I will always make the right choice, through the help of God.

Verse For Today

I have hidden your word in my heart that I might not sin against you.–Psalm 119:11

Fill It Out

Write down all the bad and negative things you need to separate or run from?	E.g. Lying
Search the Scripture and write out a verse each that can guide you to keep away from the things you mentioned above. Make every effort to reflect on the verses and apply the lessons to your life.	E.g. Lying *"The LORD detests lying lips, but He delights in those who tell the truth."—Proverbs 12:22*

DAY 4

Read Genesis 41:15–40

FROM TRASH TO TRIUMPH

Almost everyone we come across aspires to rule and reign, and we believe you also want to be in a place of authority one day. It's even a common prayer amongst believers, "Dear Lord, like Joseph, please let me reign in the palace." This is a very good prayer, but many people leave out what it takes to rule and reign. When you say that prayer, always remember to add this, *"Dear Lord, I ask that you give me the grace to go through every trash I find myself and help me by Your Spirit to keep my trust in You, so I can come out triumphantly in Jesus name."* There is no triumph without trash! Joseph was 17 years old when he had a dream, and he didn't become the Governor of Egypt until he was 30 years old. Not only did He become the governor, his entire family also came to bow to him, to show us that all his dreams came true.

Know This

It took thirteen years for Joseph's dream to come true. Yours too can take years.

Joseph's trash experiences were his preparation phase. The stage you are in right now is your preparation phase, do all the things you need to do diligently and wisely.

Dreams help us set goals, plan and prepare ahead. Dreams also help us set godly values that guide us even in difficult times.

When you are faithful in little things, God will put you in charge of greater things.

Declaration

For the Lord my God is going with me! He will fight for me against anyone who fights against me, and he will give me victory!

Verse For Today

LORD, you alone are my inheritance, my cup of blessing. You guard all that is mine. The land you have given me is a pleasant land. What a wonderful inheritance!–Psalm 16:5–6

Fill It Out

What is your big dream? It could be one thing you are so passionate about.	
Write down your plan	
Write down the actions you need to start taking	

DAY 5

Read Genesis 45:1–28

PAYING THE PRICE OF COMPASSION

Tom just moved to a new school. Suddenly, he met Luke who bullied, lied against him and allowed him to go through many years of pain in his previous school. What would you do if you were Tom? "Who are these that I am seeing? Can this be true? No, it can't be Reuben! Am I alright? But wait, if they are my brothers, I can only see ten of them, where is the eleventh?" These and more were the thoughts running through Joseph's mind. When they moved closer, he realised they were his brothers. Apparently, he must have thought they had maltreated the eleventh brother, the last born of their father.

Joseph wept! Again, what would you have done if you were in Joseph's shoes? It wasn't easy for Joseph to accept, but looking at where he had been promoted to, he could only believe it was because of God's LOVE to him. He acted like God and chose one thing–COMPASSION. With this he was able to forgive his brothers and through his influence, they were well taken care of and were also given a place to settle and expand.

Know This

Joseph was upset when he saw his brother, but he was wise enough not to allow his temper to control him. He didn't lash out curses on them, instead he went away from them to cry.

It takes time to heal from hurts, especially hurts from family members or close friends. If you need to cry please do, speak to your parents or a trusted person and above all, God, He will give you strength and wisdom to handle the situation.

Always remember this, "When you are hurting, if you hold on to it, you hurt yourself more and you may also hurt others." Therefore give up all your pains, hurts and bitterness, so you can be healed and also be a source of healing to those who hurt.

It takes compassion not to get tired of doing good, it takes compassion to love those who are mean to you, it takes compassion to forgive those who betrayed you . . . Oh! It takes compassion to use your influence to add value to the lives of those who did not only mean evil for you but also pushed you into danger.

Declaration

I receive healing for my hurting heart and I receive grace to forgive everyone that offended me in the past and those that will offend me in the future. From now on, I will be a source of healing to those who are hurting in Jesus' name.

Verse For Today

My command is this: Love each other as I have loved you. Greater love has no one than this: to lay down one's life for one's friends.–John 15:12–13

Fill It Out

Has a family member or a close friend ever done something to you that made you cry for days?	
How did you handle the situation?	
Would you have handled it better? How?	
In what way can you pay the price of compassion?	
Write a Bible verse to support your answer to the question above, memorise it, recite it and practice it regularly.	

DAY 6

Read Proverbs 31:1–9

WHY MENTORSHIP?

According to World Education Services, "Mentorship is a relationship between two people where the individual with more experience, knowledge, and connections is able to pass along what they have learned to a more junior individual within a certain field. The more senior individual is the mentor, and the more junior individual is the mentee."

Who would you think Joseph's mentor was? Jacob, his father! Jacob was a businessman who was blessed with the gift of wisdom. Because Joseph was the father's favorite, the father must have shared with him lots of experiences. Even though Joseph was only 17 years old when he was separated from his father, he had spent his childhood learning so many skills from him; leadership, administrative, wealth creation/management and character development skills. As a result of this, his determination to place faith in God and his total submission to the mentorship of the Holy Spirit (The Spirit of God), helped him to become the pride of nations.

Know This

A godly mentor intercedes for his mentees, just as Moses went to the Lord on behalf of the daughters of Zelophehad.

A mentor wants the best for you. He always looks out for the best in you and guides you along that right path you have chosen, just as King Lemuel's mother did in the Scripture you read.

A mentor gives his mentee sincere feedback, corrects and disciplines whenever necessary.

A mentor is not intimidated by the success of her mentees, he does all he could to set them up for success; encourages, affirms and celebrates them.

Some of your roles as a mentee are to be committed, humble, patient, responsive, be eager to learn, exhibit positive attitude, ask questions, share what you are up to with your mentor and above all accept godly counsel and discipline.

Declaration For Today

I have a teachable spirit and I will accept wise counsel and discipline that will guide me into becoming a well–rounded man.

Verse For Today

Remember your leaders who taught you the word of God. Think of all the good that has come from their lives, and follow the example of their faith.–Hebrews 13:7

Fill it Out

Do you have a mentor?	
In what skill do you need a mentor to guide you?	
Describe your relationship with your mentor in three words.	
Mention three things you can start doing to improve your relationship with your mentor?	

DAY 7

Reflection

COLOURFUL CHARACTER

Joseph displayed unique and notable characters that made him stand out everywhere he found himself.

He is an embodiment of:
1. **Faithfulness,** even in difficulty and when put in charge of Potiphar's household and Pharaoh's kingdom.
2. **Strength,** in times when he could have easily given up.
3. **Perseverance,** even when he was in prison for no wrong done.
4. **Goodness,** even when he knew that he might not receive the same in return, based on his previous experiences.
5. **Faith,** even when he could not see the light at the end of the tunnel.
6. **Love,** even when it was difficult to love those that

were mean to him.

7.   **Diligence,** even when he was a slave in Potiphar's house and in prison.

8.   **Wisdom,** even during a long and difficult period of famine.

Looking at these qualities, did you notice that all of them are inner qualities? Yet they were noticeable. People noticed them all in Joseph and these qualities made his character much more colorful than the coat of many colours his father gave him.

How colourful is your character? You don't have to paint them with any physical paint (like acrylic), but with the paint called the fruit of the Spirit (love, joy, peace, patience, kindness, goodness, faithfulness, gentleness and self–control). Start working on your character, adding a colour at a time.

Declaration For Today

I am full of compassion and strength, I have a teachable spirit, I am a helper and above all I live daily in the fear of God.

Verse For Today

Don't let anyone think less of you because you are young. Be an example to all believers in what you say, in the way you live, in your love, your faith, and your purity.–1 Timothy 4:12

Fill It Out

How can you use the paint called the *fruit of the Spirit* to add color to your character?	
Love	e.g. Make up my mind to love as Jesus loves, even if it is not convenient.
Love	
Joy	
Peace	
Patience	

Kindness	
Goodness	
Faithfulness	
Gentleness	
Self–control	

In Conclusion

IT WILL BE GOOD TO conclude that God does not promise any of His children a life free of troubles, but He assures us that no matter how big the trouble is, He has won the victory for us. He is not only walking alongside you, He is also ahead of you. You may not see Him at every stage but He is there holding your hand and most of the time He carries you. The grace He gives is sufficient to take you through and overcome troubles and hard times.

The troubles that come our way are but for a while, they don't last forever and your own difficult situation may be different from the other person's. A lot of boys had not only given up on God and themselves but had given up on life by committing suicide. What a pity!

What are your struggles? What are you worried about? Your identity, studies, grades, future ambition, stature, peer pressure, health challenge, insecurity, fear, doubt, addictions or what? Remain prayerful, faithful, consistent and steadfast as you follow God's plan. He is ever–faithful, ever–consistent and ever–committed to His plan for you and He will not fail to fulfil His promise at the set time. The determination to succeed, by placing bold faith in God is the key to success and it's a choice you need to make to turn your trash into triumph.

We can't wait to hear about your success story!

Testimonies
From Josephs & Daniels

JDC, the boys' mentoring group at Elegant Initiatives changed my life. Before I joined JDC, I used to lie and disobey my parents. But my life has changed since I joined and I have been introduced to daily Bible study, where I can read a chapter a day; meditate on what I learn, share insights with my friends at EI and also take actions on the lessons. I am also becoming more confident in sharing my faith in God with others.

Mitchell (8 years)

Elegant Initiatives has helped me study the Bible more, strengthen my connection with God, and helped me change my attitude to a more positive one in everything I do. EI is great, everything is well run; the morning prayers, Sunday mentoring meetings, and Tuesday book club. These activities are so great and have helped me so much. I see myself becoming a well-rounded person and I'm grateful to God.

Ireyan (11 years)

I am grateful to God for EI, which has helped me to grow close to God while I am still young and set an example for others on how a Christian lives. I have enjoyed meeting new people and making new friends, as well as learning things I never knew before in an exciting way. I have also enjoyed the opportunity to become a young leader!

Ihechi (12 years)

Parents' Testimonies

Great work God is doing through Elegant Initiatives. My Boys are becoming more conscious about themselves, their actions and how these affect their lives as a Christian and in everyday living. Their prayer lives improve and consciousness of God's existence is instilled in them. Being part of this fellowship has been a tremendous blessing!

K. Adeniran

EI has been a positive influence in the lives of our children since they joined in 2020. The requirement to read a chapter of the Bible a day and share insights has helped them become doers and not just hearers of the Word. They are developing the habit of reading the Bible daily, meditating on what they have learnt and identifying practical ways to apply it in their everyday activities. They have also been encouraged in their faith by being with their peers who love God and share the same values. EI has helped them understand and build leadership skills. My husband and I appreciate the support of the EI team in helping our children become what God wants them to be.

C. & O. Edeh

Dear Joseph,

Thank you for reading this book. Is it a blessing to you? Why not recommend it to your book club, junior church, teens gathering, friends and loved ones!

If you have also received help from this book or any of our initiatives, share your testimony and your prayer request with us by contacting the authors via any of the following means:

Write:

Tomilola Ogunkunle or
35 Goodhope Gardens
Aberdeen
AB21 9NG
United Kingdom

Joana Dzegblor
7 Nii Adjei Kwabla Avenue
Accra
GD–032–1509
Ghana

Email: admin@elegantinitiatives.com

Call: +447309255086 or +233207687649

God bless you.

Tomilola Ogunkunle & Joana Dzegblor

Books By The Authors

The Well–rounded

Have you ever wondered, "How can I grow to become a person after God's heart and the pride of nations, in a world filled with fear, rivalry, abuse and insecurity?" These tools will guide every reader to discover their purpose, identify and deal with their inadequacies and learn all that it takes to become well–rounded.

Tomilola Ogunkunle
Joana Dzegblor

Tomilola Ogunkunle

Tomilola Ogunkunle
Joana Dzegblor

Tomilola Ogunkunle

We will be looking forward to hearing your story of transformation!

OTHER INITIATIVES

Mentoring Group
Elegant Initiatives
Aberdeen, UK
www.elegantinitiatives.com

Skills & Empowerment Weekend
SEW
Worldwide

Bible Club
ACAD–A Chapter A Day
Worldwide

Book Club
Read with Tomiann
Worldwide

Fashion School
Elegant Creative Mind Academy
Aberdeen, UK
www.ecmacademy.co.uk

Printed in Great Britain
by Amazon

71848466R00129